"Charles Spurgeon is without question one of my favorite preachers of all time: profoundly Christ-centered, warmly experiential, and delightfully practical. Seldom is my soul not deeply stirred after reading and pondering one of his sermons. Of the nearly 4,000 sermons that Spurgeon preached in his lifetime, Jeff Medders has adapted 75 of Spurgeon's choice messages on the passion, death, and resurrection of Jesus into 40 savory devotionals, each of which ends with heart-searching, reflective questions and prayers which foster meditation, application, and doxology. The selections in this volume are not only ideal for preparation in the season before Easter but are applicable for every part of the year as well. I am confident that after reading this devotional, you will want more of Spurgeon—and above all, more of the Christ whom this 'prince of preachers' so beautifully proclaimed."

Joel R. Beeke, Chancellor and Professor of Homiletics & Systematic Theology, Puritan Reformed Theological Seminary

"The Christian past is ever a rich source of encouragement, instruction, challenge, and even rebuke for God's people today. And this devotional from the works of the Victorian Baptist C.H. Spurgeon, is ample proof in this regard. The preaching of Spurgeon, like that of his Particular Baptist forebears, made much of the events surrounding Easter, in which the crucified and risen Lord was revealed as humanity's one and only Savior. Pondering the selections in this devotional will surely help to deepen the reader's understanding of this revelation as well as firing the heart and will to serve such a Lord of glory!"

Michael A.G. Haykin, Professor of Church History, The Southern Baptist Theological Seminary

"This devotional is really, really good. Just when I thought I knew all of Spurgeon's gems, J.A. Medders has gone to the treasure chest and brought out some more. Read this to enjoy C.H. Spurgeon at his very best and to fix your eyes on Jesus."

Alistair Begg, Senior Pastor at Parkside Church in Cleveland, Ohio; Bible Teacher at Truth For Life

T0282031

"Few voices over the past 2,000 years have been more used by God to stir people's hearts with a greater love for Jesus than that of Charles Haddon Spurgeon. In this wonderful Easter devotional, Medders has compiled some of the best of Spurgeon's words, skilfully guiding us through the life, death, and resurrection of Christ. Here in *The Risen King*, you will find daily devotions that are brief yet rich with biblical insight; a perfect supplement to a morning Bible-reading schedule. I highly recommend this book, and I am confident that everyone who reads it will come away more amazed at the glory and goodness and grace of God."

Adam Ramsey, Lead Pastor, Liberti Church, Australia;
Director, Acts 29 Asia Pacific; Author, *Truth on Fire*

"In Jeff Medders' *The Risen King*, we have the opportunity to taste Charles Spurgeon's writings as renewed wine in new wineskins. These fresh devotionals have a high trinitarian focus and enable us to worship God in Spirit and truth while clearly pointing to Jesus, our Redeemer. Medders masterfully regenerates Spurgeon's voice with a tone refreshingly asserting that Spurgeon still speaks to us today."

Robert Smith, Jr., Distinguished Professor of Divinity,
Beeson Divinity School

"I always find myself encouraged and edified when I read Spurgeon. He rightly sees the whole Bible through single verses and skillfully combines exegesis, theology, and a pastoral heart. Medders has helpfully collected devotions from Spurgeon that lead us toward the climactic event in Jesus' life—the resurrection. Read and be enraptured by Christ through one of Christ's most gifted servants."

Patrick Schreiner, Associate Professor of New Testament and
Biblical Theology, Midwestern Baptist Theological Seminary

THE
RISEN
KING

C.H. SPURGEON

40 DEVOTIONS FOR EASTER

EDITED BY
J.A. MEDDERS

The Risen King
© J.A. Medders 2025

Published by:
The Good Book Company

thegoodbook
COMPANY

thegoodbook.com | thegoodbook.co.uk
thegoodbook.com.au | thegoodbook.co.nz | thegoodbook.co.in

Published in association with the literary agency of THE GATES GROUP

Cover design by Faceout Studio | Design and art direction by André Parker

ISBN: 9781802541298 | JOB-007968 | Printed in India

CONTENTS

PREFACE

Charles Haddon Spurgeon (1834–1892), pastor of the Metropolitan Tabernacle in London, is known as one of the most beloved pastors, writers, and preachers in the history of Christ's church. It's not because his sermons and books have sold millions of copies worldwide or because he has more words published in English than anyone else. And it's not because thousands were converted and baptized through his ministry or because he founded a college for pastors. Spurgeon is a soul-edifying read because his sermons overflow with the sweet aroma of Jesus Christ. His preaching was unparalleled in making known the glory of Christ. The grace of God is unavoidable in Spurgeon's works. Whatever the sermon, lecture, or book, Spurgeon exalted our great God and Savior. And this book is no different.

You are holding a new book from C.H. Spurgeon— at least, that's what I hope you will experience as you read. His famous devotionals—*Morning by Morning* and *Evening by Evening*—were created as summaries, excerpts, and outlines from his sermons. And it's in that same spirit that I pulled this book together from Spurgeon's sermons. When I realized that Spurgeon never created an Easter or Advent devotional, I knew one needed to be published—and it is my privilege to be a steward of Spurgeon's sermons in *The Risen King* and *The Newborn King* (due for release in 2026). I hope you will enjoy these books as though they are new works from the "Prince of Preachers."

I began this project by imagining what Spurgeon would have written and emphasized if he were the one writing. From my years of personal and doctoral work on Spurgeon, I studied the vast catalog of his sermons and selected texts and topics for the themes at hand. From these sermons, I pulled excerpts that showcased what many have come to love and expect from Spurgeon—piercing insights, vivid language, and soul-thrilling meditations on Christ's person and work. As I read sermon after sermon, I compiled entries from single or multiple sermons that fully capture Spurgeon's voice and insights on the biblical text and theme. While I did modernize language and sentence structure at spots to serve those new to Spurgeon and his Victorian English, my presence is minimal. As the editor, I wrote a clarifying or summarizing sentence for context at some points, but, rest assured, you are reading Spurgeon.

As you read *The Risen King* and journey through the Gospels this Easter season, I hope and pray that Spurgeon's devotions will help you grow in love, awe, and praise of Jesus Christ. Every entry is a billboard to the greatness of Jesus. Look to him. Worship your Savior with every ounce of your heart. Let's say together as Christ's people, "Long live the risen King!"

Happy Easter,
Jeff Medders

DAY 1

Behold!

The next day he saw Jesus coming toward him, and said, "Behold, the Lamb of God, who takes away the sin of the world!"

JOHN 1:29

Lifting up his hand and pointing to Jesus, John the Baptist cried, "Behold the Lamb of God, who takes away the sin of the world." He did not say, *Behold the great Example.* He did not even say, *Behold the king and leader of a new era.* The first point that he dwells upon, and which wins his enthusiasm, is "the Lamb of God." John the Baptist views Christ as the propitiation, the atoning sacrifice, for sin.

Notice how John says, "Behold the Lamb of God." This is different from what John would have said about all the lambs that he had ever heard or read of since the first appointment of sacrifice. He remembered the first of the flock which Abel offered and the sweet-smelling sacrifice which Noah presented. He knew the sacrifices of Abraham, Isaac, and Jacob. He was familiar with the lamb of the Passover supper and those of Israel's high festivals. He remembered the thousands of offerings that had been presented by David and by Solomon, and by other kings in the great national acts of worship. But passing them by as if they were all mere shadows, he points his finger to the man Christ Jesus, and he says of him, *This is the Lamb of God.*

What does the Lamb do? What blessed words—he "takes away" our sin! Where did he take it? I will tell you: "As far as the east is from the west, so far does he remove our transgressions from us" (Psalm 103:12). He took the sin of all believers away so completely that it sank into the bottom of the sea. God has cast it behind his back, and it will not be mentioned against us any more forever. There is no such thing now as the sin of the saints—Christ has utterly annihilated it. He came to finish transgression and to make an end of sins. And if he made an end of them, they are gone forever.

So John calls us to "behold the Lamb of God"— is that all the sinner has to do? Yes, behold him. The mere looking at him saves the soul. Whosoever looks to Christ lives by that look and shall live forever. All who are in heaven entered there simply through beholding the slain Lamb, who takes away the sin of the world. There is life in a look at the Lamb of God. Look even out of the corner of your eye if that is all that you can do! Look through your blinding tears!

John the Baptist's one business was to bear witness to

Christ. He was the morning star which heralds the rising sun. When the sun appeared, he had no more reason for shining. You cannot account for John except by Jesus—the one reason for John's existence is Jesus.

I wish it might be so with us. May we be able to say, "For me to live is Christ" (Philippians 1:21). May our lives be such that they cannot be understood apart from Jesus. May it be the case that if we were to take him away, our whole character would become an inexplicable mystery. I am afraid that some professing Christians could be easily interpreted apart from Christ. But if we are like John, true witnesses to Jesus, we shall find in Jesus the conscious purpose of our being, and his glory will be the clue to all the windings of our lives. For this purpose we were born, and for this end we have come into the world: that we may bear witness to the Lord Jesus Christ. Search and look, my brothers and sisters, to see whether it is so with you.

REFLECT

How are you making it your business to behold the Lord Jesus and bear witness to him? How can you behold Jesus through your day today? And for whom will you pray, that you have an opportunity to share Jesus with them?

PRAY

What a comfort to know that my sins have been taken away by the you, the Lamb of God. Warm my heart with the good news of the gospel. May the joy of the gospel run so hot in my heart that it overflows in raising my voice to tell others what the Lamb of God does for us weary sinners. Thank you, Jesus. Amen.

DAY 2

The Beloved Son

And when Jesus was baptized, immediately he went up from the water, and behold, the heavens were opened to him, and he saw the Spirit of God descending like a dove and coming to rest on him; and behold, a voice from heaven said, "This is my beloved Son, with whom I am well pleased."

MATTHEW 3:16-17

In our text, we find that the Father not only calls Christ his Son, but he says, "This is my beloved Son." What wondrous love there must be in the heart of each of the divine Persons in the sacred Trinity towards each other! How blessedly they must look upon one another with divine favor and pleasure! There could never be any division in their interests, for they are one in heart, one in purpose, one in every respect. As Jesus said, "I and the Father are one" (John 10:30).

We glean from this text how God not only calls Christ his beloved Son but says he is well pleased with him.

And if you are so united to Christ as to be one with him, God will also be well pleased with you for his dear Son's sake. But can a sinner ever be pleasing to God? Not in himself or herself, apart from Christ. But all who are in Christ are accepted "in the Beloved" (Ephesians 1:6). The Father is so pleased with Jesus that all whom he represents are pleasing to God for his sake.

Maybe you are asking, "But how can I be in Christ?" My dear friend, if you are one of the Lord's chosen, you are already in Christ in God's eternal purpose. But the way in which you must get into Christ is by true faith in him. To trust in Jesus is to be in Jesus. To rely upon the atoning sacrifice of Christ is to be one with Christ. Faith is the uniting bond which binds together the Christ in whom we believe and those who believe in him.

It does not take the Holy Spirit an hour to convert a soul. The vital spark that regenerates a soul is kindled in an instant. If you are truly trusting in Christ, God looks upon you as a part of Christ's mystical body, and he is well pleased with you for Christ's sake. Then, you have the Son suffering for you, the Spirit applying to you the merit of his atoning sacrifice, and the Father well pleased with you because you are trusting in his beloved Son. Or to put the truth in another form, the Father gives the great gospel feast, the Son is the feast, and the Spirit not only brings the invitations, but he also gathers the guests around the table. Or, to use another metaphor, God the Father is the fountain of grace, God the Son is the channel of grace, and God the Holy Spirit is the cup from which we drink of the flowing stream. Eat and drink!

REFLECT

How do you view yourself? Do you think of your heavenly Father as being pleased when he sees you? Where are you battling to believe what God sees and says about you in Christ?

PRAY

What a delight to see and hear the intra-trinitarian love on display as the Son was baptized! And what a delight of grace to be welcomed into this love. Thank you, Father, for calling me your child. Thank you, Jesus, for loving me as your brother or sister. Thank you, Holy Spirit, for the seal of redeeming love. I want to feast on this love today. In your name, Jesus. Amen.

DAY 3

Tempted in the Wilderness

Then Jesus was led up by the Spirit into the
wilderness to be tempted by the devil. And after
fasting forty days and forty nights, he was hungry.

MATTHEW 4:1-2

The Savior's public life begins and ends with temptation.

It commences in the wilderness in a close contest with satanic craftiness, and it ends in Gethsemane in a dreadful battle with the powers of darkness. There are a few bright spots between, but the gloom of the desert deepens into the midnight darkness of the cross as if to show to us that we also must begin with trial and must reckon upon ending with it.

Martin Luther learned the art of spiritual navigation from having done business himself in deep waters of spiritual tribulation. Luther's remark stands true: that prayer, meditation, and temptation are the three best instructors of the gospel believer, and since I have lately experienced much of the latter, I must use what I have learned. But whatever we do, we shall be tempted.

God had one Son without sin, but he never had a son without temptation. The natural man or woman is born to trouble as the sparks fly upward (Job 5:7), and the Christian is born to temptation just as certainly and necessarily. It is our duty to be always on our watch against Satan because we do not know when he will come.

He is like a thief, and he gives no hint of his approach. Like the assassin, he will sneak upon his victim. If Satan always acted aboveboard—if he were a bold and open adversary—we might deal with him. But because he meets us unawares and besets us in dark and miry places on the way, we need to pray against temptation, and we need to hear the Savior's admonition, *What I say to you, I say to all: Watch.*

If you know anything of the spiritual life, you will have observed that the most likely times for Satan to attack a Christian are those they deem unlikely. In such an hour as you think he will not, the prince of this world comes. Just when you would say, "I am safe," then it is that you are in danger. Beware, dear friends, of the devil; beware of him most when you think you have least need to beware of him. And be all the more aware of your Christ, the one who defeated the devil.

REFLECT

What are the areas of your life where the temptations to sin are strong? Where do you need to call upon Christ today? Is there any situation about which you might be in danger of spiritual complacency where instead you may need to be on your guard?

PRAY

Lord, as I walk through the valley of the shadow of death, as temptations swirl around me, keep my eyes upon you. Your victory over Satan is my victory. Keep me watchful, Holy Spirit. May the light of your word brighten the darkness that hides Satan's traps and schemes. Lead me, guide me, and help me, Lord Jesus. In your name, I pray. Amen.

DAY 4

Repentance Is Never Out of Fashion

From that time Jesus began to preach, saying,
"Repent, for the kingdom of heaven is at hand."

MATTHEW 4:17

... and that repentance for the forgiveness
of sins should be proclaimed in his name to
all nations, beginning from Jerusalem.

LUKE 24:47

Jesus begins his mission crying, "Repent" (Mark 1:15). And he ends it by saying to his successors, the apostles, "that repentance for the forgiveness of sins should be proclaimed in his name to all nations, beginning from Jerusalem." This seems to me to be not simply an interesting fact but instructive. With this he begins, and with this he will conclude. He knew that repentance was, to spiritual life, a sort of Alpha and Omega—it was the duty of the beginning; it was the duty of the end.

True repentance consists of illumination, humiliation, detestation, and transformation. Repentance sighs over the sin—confession tells it out. Repentance feels the sin to be heavy within—confession plucks it forth and lays it before the throne of God. Repentance is the soul in stress—confession delivers it. Through repentance, my heart is ready to burst, and there is a fire in my bones—confession gives the heavenly fire a vent, and my soul flames upward before God. Repentance alone has groanings which cannot be uttered—confession is the voice which expresses the groans.

Repentance clears away the rubbish of the past temple of sin. Holiness builds the new temple which the Lord our God shall inherit. Repentance and the desire for holiness can never be separated. Sin is such a troublesome companion that it will always give you heartache till you have turned it out through repentance. And then your heart shall rest and be still. Sin is the rough wind that tears through the forest and sways every branch of the trees to and fro. But after repentance has come into the soul, the wind is hushed, and all is still, and the birds sing in the branches of the trees which just now creaked in the storm. Repentance ever yields sweet peace to those who possess it.

I am a living witness that repentance is exceedingly sweet when mixed with divine hope. But repentance without hope is hell. It is hell to grieve for sin with the pangs of bitter remorse and yet to know that pardon can never come and mercy can never be granted. Repentance, with the cross before its eyes, is heaven itself.

Repentance, then, has this excellency: that it is very sweet to the soul which is made to lie beneath its shadow. When the blood of Jesus is sprinkled on a repentant heart, even the songs of the angels and the vials full of sweet odors that smoke before the throne of the Most High are not more agreeable to God than the sighs and groans and tears of the brokenhearted repentant soul. So then, if you desire to please God, come before him with many and many a tear. "A broken and contrite heart, O God, you will not despise" (Psalm 51:17).

REFLECT

What do you need to repent of today? What do you need to confess before God? How can you enjoy his peace?

PRAY

Father, teach me to prize repentance to the same degree that I did on the first day of salvation. Restore to me the desire, enjoyment, and watchfulness that is needed for ongoing repentance. Reveal any unclean way in me—so I can see the blood of Jesus over my sin and learn to walk upright again. Help me, Holy Spirit, I pray, in the name of Jesus. Amen.

DAY 5

Christ Lifted Up

*And as Moses lifted up the serpent in the
wilderness, so must the Son of Man be lifted up,
that whoever believes in him may have eternal life.*

JOHN 3:14-15

I must admit that, at first sight, the bronze serpent
seems to be the most absurd invention that anyone
could have devised for curing those who were bitten.
Yet, I see in the bronze serpent, when I come to study
it, the highest wisdom that even God himself could develop. "So Moses made a bronze serpent and set it on a
pole. And if a serpent bit anyone, he [or she] would look
at the bronze serpent and live" (Numbers 21:9). Our
texts say that Moses lifted it up upon a pole, and, with
one look, life was given. Ah, dear friends, Christ Jesus
must be lifted up for those who are bitten by sin and lie
in terminal danger so that we may live.

"Oh," says the sinner, "I have been so sinful! I can't be
saved." What has the extent of your sin to do with it?

Christ is infinitely righteous—look at him. "No, no," says another, "I cannot look at Christ. You do not know what crimes I have committed. I have been a drunk, I have been enslaved to lust, and more. How can I be saved!?" My dear reader, your wounds have nothing to do with it. Christ on the cross is all you need—all you have to do is to look.

For remember, the brazen serpent was lifted up so that everyone in the camp who was bitten might live. And now Christ is lifted up to you so that "whoever believes in him should not perish but have eternal life" (John 3:16). The devil says that you are shut out; tell him that "whoever" shuts out none. Oh, that precious word: "whoever." Remember, the serpents bit everyone—it didn't matter how old they were or where they lived in the camp—but if they looked, they lived. Remember, it is the same Christ for big sinners as for little sinners, for gray heads as for babies, for the poor as for the rich, for chimney sweeps as for monarchs, and it is the same Christ for prostitutes as for saints—"whoever."

If you are weeping today on account of your sin, look to Jesus. And for your encouragement, note first that Jesus Christ was put on the cross on purpose for you to look at. Look at him. Look at him, and live. Remember again for your encouragement that he asks you to look. He invites you to believe. The promises of Jesus Christ are all as good as oaths—they never fail. He says, "whoever believes in him should not perish but have eternal life." Just cast yourself wholly on Christ, and if you are not saved, then God's book is a lie, and God himself has broken his truth. But that cannot be! Come and try it. Look to him!

REFLECT

How can you look upon Christ today? What sins can you hold forward and then look at Jesus and believe you are forgiven and healed?

PRAY

Lord Jesus, you were lifted up for me—and I lift you up in praise and adoration. You took on the curse so I could take on the blessing. I look to you today, depending on you and loving you. Praise you, Jesus, for your grace and mercy towards me. Amen.

DAY 6

For God So Loved

*For God so loved the world, that he gave his
only Son, that whoever believes in him should
not perish but have eternal life. For God did
not send his Son into the world to condemn
the world, but in order that the world might
be saved through him. Whoever believes in
him is not condemned, but whoever does not
believe is condemned already, because he has not
believed in the name of the only Son of God.*

JOHN 3:16-18

This text is the whole Bible in miniature. We may
speak of these verses in so many words and so many
volumes, for every single syllable here is charged to the
full with meaning. We may read it and reread it, and
still continue to read it day and night, yet ever find
some fresh instruction in it. Why? It is the essence of the
gospel—the good news in brief. So, I invite those of you
that have long known your Lord to take up your first

spelling book and go over your ABCs again, by learning that God so loved the world that he gave his Son to die, that we might live through him.

I do not call you to an elementary lesson because you have forgotten your letters but because it is a good thing to refresh the memory and a blessed thing to feel young again. I call you back to the cross and to him who bled there for you. It is a good thing for us all to return at times to our starting place and make sure that we are following the way everlasting. It is wise to come to him afresh, as we came on that first day when we were helpless, needy, and heavy-laden, and we stood weeping at the cross and left our burden at the pierced feet. There we learned to look and live and love from the love of God.

If you desire to see the love of God, you must consider how he gave his Son. He did not give his Son, as you might do, in pursuit of some profession in which you might still enjoy his company. He gave his Son to exile among men and women. He sent him down to that distant manger, and there he slept, where horned oxen fed! The Lord God sent the heir of all things to toil in a carpenter's shop: to drive the nail and push the plane and use the saw. He sent him down among scribes and Pharisees, whose cunning eyes watched him and whose cruel tongues scourged him with base slanders. He sent him down to hunger and thirst amid poverty so dire that he had nowhere to lay his head. He sent him down to the scourging and the crowning with thorns, to the giving of his back to the whips and his cheeks to those that plucked off the hair. At length, he gave him up to death—a felon's death, the death of the crucified. Behold that cross and see the anguish of him that dies upon it. His cry of "Lema sabachthani ... why have you forsaken me?" (Matthew 27:46) tells us how fully God gave his Son to ransom the souls of the sinful. He gave him to be made a curse for us—gave him that he might die "the righteous for the unrighteous, that he might bring us to God" (1 Peter 3:18). Oh, wondrous stretch of love that Jesus Christ should die!

He is God's free gift to all free receivers. A full Christ for empty sinners. If you can but hold out your empty willing hand, the Lord will give Christ to you at this moment. Nothing is freer than a gift.

REFLECT

How real is the love of God to you today? How affected are you by the magnitude of God in giving his Son for you, for the cross, for your sins? What comfort do you find in knowing that Christ, while fully God, lived a fully human life for you?

PRAY

Holy God, help me to see the love that radiates from your heart to me today: past and present and future love all displayed at the cross. Revive my heart around the simple and supernatural message of the gospel—Christ for me. In the mighty name of Jesus. Amen.

DAY 7

True Holy Water

Jesus said to her, "Everyone who drinks of this water will be thirsty again, but whoever drinks of the water that I will give him will never be thirsty again. The water that I will give him will become in him a spring of water welling up to eternal life." The woman said to him, "Sir, give me this water, so that I will not be thirsty or have to come here to draw water."

JOHN 4:13-15

True religion is a gift from Jesus. Our Lord says, "The water that I will give him [or her]." The only true religion in the world is that which comes from Jesus Christ, and the only fulfillment of that true religion in your own soul is by receiving it from the hand of Christ. True spiritual life, in all its details, is connected with him. Do we want peace of conscience because sin is forgiven? We have redemption through his blood, the forgiveness of sins. Do we desire deliverance from the power of sin within us? We can only overcome by the blood of the Lamb. Do we need teaching? The best instruction comes from his lips. Do we desire an example which will empower us to obey the teaching? He is our pattern: "Christ Jesus, who became to us wisdom from God, righteousness and sanctification and redemption" (1 Corinthians 1:30). He is our all in all. If anyone dreams they have a God-given religion, they are in deadly error if the mark of the pierced hand is not upon it. That peace which does not come to us sealed with the blood of the Mediator's sacrifice is a false peace. You must drink from the fountain opened upon Calvary. Drink from the cup which Jesus fills; do not think that satisfying waters can be drawn from any well but him.

True godliness is next described in the text as a gift which must be received: "Whoever drinks of the water that I will give him..." It is received, you see, not merely into the hand but into the inward parts. When we drink water, it enters into us, saturates us, becomes a part of our being, and helps to build up the fabric of our body. And so, we must receive Jesus Christ into our innermost self, not professing to believe with the creed of the head while the heart remains in unbelief. We cannot give our Lord the empty compliment of praising his character while we reject his mission. True religion is trusting him, depending upon him, loving him, following him, yielding ourselves to him, living upon him, living in him— that it may be clear that he has entered into and become one with us forever. We need Christ in us: Christ in the secret fountain of our being.

What we want is not Jesus Christ pictured on the wall nor his name on the lip nor words about him from pious books. We want the Lord himself received into our heart: "Christ in you, the hope of glory" (Colossians 1:27). Oh, would Christ live, dwell, and reign within our entire nature, looking out from our eyes, speaking by our lips, blessing the poor by our hands, going about doing good with our feet, and magnifying God in these mortal bodies as once he did on earth in his own body. This is true religion: Jesus Christ received by an act of faith into our innermost soul. Dear friend, have you got this? Before we go an inch further, let every man and woman press this question home: do I know what it is to drink of the life-giving stream which Jesus Christ bestows?

REFLECT

What fruits do you see in your life of enjoying and depending upon Christ? How are you drinking this living water, which he gives into your soul?

PRAY

Lord, only you can give me the true life that I need. May I never be diagnosed with spiritual dehydration. Your living water will satisfy my soul. Help me to reject all other brands, all other water enhancers, and depend solely upon you. Quench the thirst in my soul, Lord. Amen.

DAY 8

Joining Christ's Mission

*And he said to them, "Follow me, and I
will make you fishers of men." Immediately
they left their nets and followed him.*

MATTHEW 4:19-20

When Christ calls us by his grace, we ought not only to remember what we are, but we also ought to think of what he can make us. Jesus starts by saying, "Follow me, and I will make you..." We should repent of what we have been but rejoice in what we may be. It is not *Follow me because of what you are already.* It is not *Follow me because you may make something of yourselves*, but *Follow me because of what I will make you.* It did not seem likely that lowly fishermen would develop into apostles—that men who were so handy with the net would be quite as much at home in preaching sermons and in instructing converts—yet that is exactly what Christ brought about. And when we are brought low in the sight of God by a sense of our own unworthiness, we

35

may feel encouraged to follow Jesus because of what he can make us.

Our Lord's metaphor is filled with lessons for our evangelistic task. The work of a fisherman is difficult. A fisherman is a person who is very dependent. He or she cannot see the fish. One who fishes in the sea must go and cast in the net without knowing what, if anything, will be caught. Fishing is an act of faith. Fishermen must be hard workers. They do not sit in an armchair and catch fish. They have to go out in rough weather. If we never do any work for Christ except when we feel up to the mark, we shall not do much. We must be always at it until we wear ourselves out, throwing our whole soul into the work, in all weathers, for Christ's sake. The winds of providence will waft you where you can fish for men and women. You will often be surprised to find how God has been in a house that you visit—before you get there, his hand has been at work in its rooms. When you wish to speak to some particular person, God's providence has been dealing with that person to make them ready for just that word which you could say—that which nobody else but you could say. Oh, be following Christ, and you will find that he will, by every experience through which you are passing, make you "fishers of men."

There are many movements from God's Spirit which are not noticed by Christians when they are in a callous condition. But when the heart is right with God and living in communion with God, we feel a sacred sensitivity so that we do not need the Lord to shout, but even his faintest whisper is heard. I do not say that the Spirit of God will certainly say to your ear, "Go over and join this chariot" (Acts 8:29). But yet, in your soul, as distinctly as the Spirit spoke to Philip, you shall hear the Lord's will. As soon as you see an individual, the thought shall cross your mind, *Go and speak to that person.* The Spirit will lead you to river or sea where you can cast your net and be a "fisher of men."

Live with Jesus and follow Jesus, and he will make you a fisher of men, women, children, friends, family, and foes. A Christian should be a bound apprentice to Jesus to learn the trade of the Savior. See how Jesus saves, and you will learn how the thing is done.

REFLECT

Where has God's providence taken you so you can cast your net and win souls for Christ? In what ways can you tune in to the Spirit's leading and follow the call of God as you go about your day?

PRAY

Lord Jesus, teach me how to be a fisher of men and women. I don't want my discipleship with you to consist only of right doctrine and right living that never leads to right evangelism. Holy Spirit, make me sensitive to your leadings and promptings to share the gospel and invite sinners to Christ, for your glory, I pray. Amen.

DAY 9

The Lord's Prayer

Our Father in heaven,
hallowed be your name.
Your kingdom come,
your will be done,
on earth as it is in heaven.
Give us this day our daily bread,
and forgive us our debts,
as we also have forgiven our debtors.
And lead us not into temptation,
but deliver us from evil.

MATTHEW 6:9-13

This prayer of Christ is a great chart, but I cannot cross the sea on a chart. It is a map, but no one is a traveler because they place their fingers across the map. And so, someone may use this form of prayer, and yet be a total stranger to the great design of Christ in teaching it to his disciples. By frequent repetitions of this blessed model, the Lord's Prayer, some seem to think that there is a magical charm in that sacred arrangement of words. But I tell you solemnly, you might as well repeat this perfect prayer backwards as forwards if your heart is not in it. Do not make praying a piece of witchcraft and your supplications an imitation of the abracadabra of the wizard, or else it is vain superstition and not acceptable supplication.

Do you, my dear readers, pray so as to speak with God? Think how you would like your own child every morning to come to you and repeat a certain set of words without meaning anything. You would say, "There, child, there, I have heard that often enough. Come to me no more with your empty noise." You would not care for vain repetitions. But when your boy or girl says, "Father, Mother, I need such a thing; please give it to me," you listen to the child's words. "That is right, dear child. Is there anything else you want? Tell me what it is. I will gladly give you all things that you need." If your prayer does not come from your heart, it will not go to God's heart. And if it does not bring you near to God, so that you are speaking to him, you have simply wasted your breath.

There should be a holy hunger and thirst to pray, and the soul never prays so well as when it is reminded by its real needs. If there be any difficulty in our minds, let us ask, for the Holy Spirit can solve it. If there be any need in our homes, let us ask, for our heavenly Father can supply it. If there be any weakness in our spiritual nature, let us ask, for God can strengthen us. If there be any longing desire of our soul which leads to great heaviness of spirit, let us ask, for our desire can be granted if it is a right one, and our heaviness can be removed.

The Lord has not only taught us to pray, but he has also given us the Holy Spirit to help our infirmities, and to make intercession for us with groanings which cannot be uttered. Do not despise using the "Lord's Prayer." It is matchless. And if we must have forms of prayer, let us have this first, foremost, and the chief. But let no one think that Christ would tie his disciples to the constant and only use of this. Let us rather draw near to the throne of heavenly grace with boldness, as children coming to a father, and let us tell our wants and our sorrows in the language which the Holy Spirit teaches us. I reckon that the Lord's Prayer is never out of date.

REFLECT
Are your prayers mere rehearsals of cold doctrine, or are they genuinely directed from your heart to God's? What difficulties, needs, weaknesses, or worries can you bring to God's ears today?

PRAY
Use the Lord's Prayer as a launching point for your own prayer.

DAY 10

Hear and Do

*Everyone then who hears these words of mine
and does them will be like a wise man who built
his house on the rock. And the rain fell, and the
floods came, and the winds blew and beat on
that house, but it did not fall, because it had
been founded on the rock. And everyone who
hears these words of mine and does not do them
will be like a foolish man who built his house
on the sand. And the rain fell, and the floods
came, and the winds blew and beat against that
house, and it fell, and great was the fall of it.*

MATTHEW 7:24-27

These were the closing words of our Savior's most famous Sermon on the Mount. The whole of his hill-sermon was intensely earnest, and that earnestness was sustained to the end, so that the closing words are like glowing coals or sharp arrows of the bow. Our Lord closes not by displaying his own powers of speech but by simply and affectionately giving a warning to those who, having heard his words, are satisfied with only hearing and not putting them into practice.

Consider these two houses. The main difference between them was not in their walls or roofs, nor in the cheapness or speed of construction. The main difference was out of sight, underground. It was all a matter of foundation.

Outward appearance is everything with people but nothing with God. The essential difference between the true child of God and the one who merely professes faith is not readily discovered, even by spiritual minds. But the Lord sees it. It is a secret, mysterious something which the Lord prizes, "for the Lord knows those who are his" (2 Timothy 2:19). Sincere trust in Jesus Christ is counterfeited in a thousand ways and often imitated so accurately that you will only discover the fraudulence by rigid self-examination. You must lie flat upon Christ, the Rock. You must depend entirely upon him; all your hope and all your trust must be in him. Beware of gathering a fictitious religion—borrowing your experience from biographies, picking up godliness second-hand from your mothers and fathers and friends and acquaintances. Whatever it may cost you of heartbreak and agony, see to it that the sure foundation is reached and the house so built that it will endure the trials which will inevitably test it. I would gladly saturate my writing with tears, so weighty and so essential do I feel this caution to be, both to myself and you.

The Christian rests peacefully upon Christ. Troubles

come one after another, but they do not sweep us away; they only endear to us the hope which is based upon Christ Jesus. And when at last death comes—that awful flood which will undermine everything that is removable—it cannot find anything to shake in the wise builder's hope. We rest on what Christ has done; death cannot affect it. We believe in a faithful God, and dying cannot affect that. We believe in the covenant signed and sealed and sanctioned—Christians hold on to the "shalls" and "wills" of an immutable God, all sealed with the blood of the Redeemer; death cannot affect any of these. No matter what is faced, the Christian lives on the Rock, in the Redeemer, with his word.

REFLECT

Where do you need to experience the peace of Christ? Are there any areas of your life where you are merely hearing and not applying God's word? How can you turn your response into doing?

PRAY

Lord, you are my Rock. Help me to obey your words. When the rains hit the house—when suffering and trials wreck the flower-filled gardens—I know I'm safe with you. My eternity is as secure as you. Comfort me today, Lord. In your name, Jesus. Amen.

DAY 11

Forgiveness First

*And behold, some people brought to him a
paralytic, lying on a bed. And when Jesus saw
their faith, he said to the paralytic, "Take heart,
my son; your sins are forgiven." And behold,
some of the scribes said to themselves, "This
man is blaspheming." But Jesus, knowing their
thoughts, said, "Why do you think evil in your
hearts? For which is easier, to say, 'Your sins
are forgiven,' or to say, 'Rise and walk'? But
that you may know that the Son of Man has
authority on earth to forgive sins"—he then
said to the paralytic—"Rise, pick up your bed
and go home." And he rose and went home.*

MATTHEW 9:2-7

The bearers of the man affected by paralysis broke
through the tiling—whatever that may have been—
to get him near the Savior. They had lowered him down
over the heads of the eager gathering, and there he lay

upon his pallet before Christ, unable to stir hand or foot but looking up with that gaze of eager expectancy which Christ so well understood.

Christ dealt first with the chief evil which afflicted this man. His paralysis would, secondarily, be a fountain of bitter grief to the sick man, and, therefore, the Savior dealt with it in the second place. But, first and foremost, over and above all grief for his infirmity, was his painful sense of unforgiven sin. Christ did not begin by curing him of the paralysis. That was bad enough, but sin in the heart is worse than paralysis of every single muscle.

At the very beginning of this miracle, to show his lordship and his royal and divine power, Christ said to the man, "Take heart, my son; your sins are forgiven" (v 2). How I love to think of the blessed fact that Christ does not forgive us and then keep his forgiveness in the dark. He says, "Son; your sins are forgiven." He gives the assurance of forgiveness to the sinner whom he forgives! The realization of pardon is a delightful feeling. Oh, if there is a joy outside of heaven that is higher than all others, it is the joy of a sinful soul when divine forgiveness is granted. I think that people would readily give up all the pleasures of this world and count them as nothing if they could but know the bliss of forgiven sin. Our Lord Jesus Christ makes us drink of the sweetness of forgiveness. It is not merely that he burns the books that recorded our debts; he also tells us he has done so. "Your sins are forgiven." It is Christ's business to pardon. It is his bliss to pardon.

It is his glory to pardon. He came here on purpose that he might pardon the guilty. Oh, that all sinful ones would go to him for forgiveness!

This is how Christ behaves towards us poor, paralyzed, sin-bound men and women. He sees our faith, and then puts our sin away where it shall be seen no more forever, for he is a King, he is God, and he is able to forgive and blot out all iniquity. I heard of one man, having been under a great sense of sin and being relieved of it, who for a long time could only cry out, "He is a great Forgiver." When there were other things to be attended to, he could not see to them or speak of any other kind of business but this: "He is a great Forgiver." I hope every reader will join me in saying, "He is a great Forgiver." And all who will trust his great atoning sacrifice shall also know that he is a great Forgiver.

REFLECT

Are you enjoying the delight of forgiveness? What past sin is haunting, nagging, and gnawing at you? Let Jesus' words heal you.

PRAY

Lord Jesus, help me remember the sweetness of known forgiveness. Grow me in the awareness of my sins being forgiven. Make sin bitter and distasteful to my soul, Holy Spirit. May I taste and see your goodness today, God. In Jesus' name. Amen.

DAY 12

The Miracle of Conversion

*As Jesus passed on from there, he saw a man called
Matthew sitting at the tax booth, and he said to
him, "Follow me." And he rose and followed him.*

MATTHEW 9:9

Matthew wrote this verse about himself. I picture
him, with his pen in hand, writing all the rest
of this Gospel, but I can imagine that when he came
to this very personal passage, he laid the pen down a
minute and wiped his eyes. This verse reads to me so
tenderly that I do not know how to communicate to
you just how I feel about it. I have tried to imagine
myself as Matthew writing this story but I am sure that
I would never have done it so beautifully as he has, for
it is so full of everything that is touching, tender, true,
and gracious.

Please notice—perhaps you did in yesterday's reading
and today's—where Matthew has put this story. It is
placed immediately after miracle of the man affected by

paralysis. It seems very beautiful on Matthew's part to record his call just here. *There*, he said, *I will tell them one miracle about the Savior having made the man with paralysis take up his bed and walk, and then I will tell them of another miracle—a greater miracle still: how there was another man who was more than paralyzed—chained to his gains—yet who, nevertheless, at the command of Christ, quit that occupation and all his gains that he might follow his Divine Master.*

You too, dear friend, can trace a parallel between your conversion and some miracle of the Master. Was it, in your case, the casting out of demons? Was it the opening of the eyes of the blind? Was it the unstopping of deaf ears and the loosing of a silent tongue? Was it the raising of the dead or, even more than that, was it the calling forth of death itself out of the grave, as when Jesus cried, "Lazarus, come out" (John 11:43) and Lazarus came forth? In any case, I invite you who know the Lord, in the silence of your souls, to sit down and think not about Matthew but about yourselves.

I shall think about a man called Spurgeon. If the Lord has looked upon you in love, you can put your own name into the text, and say, "As Jesus passed on from there, he saw a man called James or John or Oliver," and you sisters may put in your names, too: Natalie and Ivy and so forth. Just sit and think how Jesus said to each one of you, "Follow me," and how, in that happy moment, you did arise and follow him.

O my dear reader, if you have been converted, it may be that something like this was true in your case! At any rate, this I know is true—you were not the first to seek Christ, but Christ was the first to seek you. You were a wandering sheep, and did not love the fold, but his sweet mercy went out after you. His grace made you thoughtful and led you to pray. The Holy Spirit breathed in you your first breath of spiritual life, and so you came to Christ. See, then, the freeness of the grace of God, the sovereignty of his choice. Admire it in the man named Matthew. Admire it still more in yourself, whatever your name may be.

REFLECT

What biblical account serves as a parallel to your conversion to Christ? How can you praise him for finding you?

PRAY

King Jesus, the fact you called my name is a wonder of grace. To others, I'm a face in the crowd, but to you, my name is graven on your hands. My name is in the Lamb's book of life (see Revelation 21:27). There is no one like you, Lord! I praise your name, Jesus. Amen.

DAY 13

A Friend of Sinners

*The Son of Man came eating and drinking,
and they say, "Look at him! A glutton and
a drunkard, a friend of tax collectors and
sinners!" Yet wisdom is justified by her deeds.*

MATTHEW 11:19

The enemies of our Lord Jesus Christ thought to brand him with infamy, hold him up to derision, and hand his name down to everlasting scorn as "a friend of tax collectors and sinners." Shortsighted mortals! To this day, the Savior is adored by the title which was designed as a slur. But troubled consciences have found a sweet balm in the very sound. Jesus, "a friend of tax collectors and sinners," has proved himself friendly to them, and they have become friends with him.

Some people like to appear as having philanthropic love toward fallen sinners, yet they would not touch them with a pair of tongs. Not so the Savior. He eats and drinks with sinners. Beloved, this is a sweet trait found in Christ and proves how real and how true his love was, that he made his associations with sinners and did not shun even the chief of them.

So fond was he of sinners that he made his grave with the wicked (Isaiah 53:9). He was numbered with the transgressors (v 12). God's fiery sword is drawn to strike a world of sinners down to hell. It must fall on those sinners. But Christ loves them. What is to be done? By what means can they be rescued? The "friend of sinners" has put himself into the sinner's place! And then, as if he has been the sinner—though in him is no sin—he suffers, bleeds, and dies: supernatural suffering, redemptive bleeding, and a substitutionary death.

It was a death in which the second death of hell was in view—a bleeding in which the very veins of God were emptied. The God-man divinely suffered. The eternal wrath of God was condensed and put into a cup, too bitter for mortal tongue to know, and then drained to its utmost dregs by the loving lips of Jesus. Beloved, this was love: "But God shows his love for us in that while we were still sinners, Christ died for us" (Romans 5:8); "Greater love has no one than this, that someone lay down his life for his friends" (John 15:13). His work has shown his friendship with us sinners.

Beloved, I cannot tell you all that Christ has done for sinners, but this I know: he will stand by you to the end. You will be hard at work today, but as you wipe the sweat from your brow, he will stand by you. You will, perhaps, be despised for his sake, but he will not forsake you. You will vex him much and grieve his Spirit. You will often doubt him—you will go after other lovers. You will provoke him to jealousy, but he will never cease to love you. You will, perhaps, grow cold toward him and even forget his dear name for a time, but he will never forget you. You may, perhaps, dishonor his cross and damage his fair fame among others, but he will never cease to love you. He will never love you less, and he cannot love you more. He is always a friend of sinners.

REFLECT

What aspect of Jesus' friendship is precious to you today? How do you think you could more deeply enjoy his friendship? Is there a fresh sin you need to bring to the friend of sinners?

PRAY

Thank you, Lord, for being a friend of sinners. I would not have sought you as a friend, but you sought me. You will be my friend and Lord forever, no matter what I confess to you today. May our friendship bring change in my life. In your name, Jesus—the friend of sinners. Amen.

DAY 14

The Heart of Jesus

Come to me, all who labor and are heavy laden,
and I will give you rest. Take my yoke upon you,
and learn from me, for I am gentle and lowly
in heart, and you will find rest for your souls.
For my yoke is easy, and my burden is light.

MATTHEW 11:28-30

This verse is one of those great wells of salvation from which we may always draw, for we can never exhaust it. The more we draw from such a text as this, the sweeter and fuller its meaning appears to us.

It is very remarkable that the only passage in the whole New Testament in which the heart of Jesus is distinctly mentioned is the one before us. In his being gentle, we see that his strength is quiet forbearance and patient endurance. His mightiest force is the sweet attraction of compassion and love. In his being lowly, which means "near the ground," we learn the posture of Christ's heart. We cannot be so low that he will not stoop to reach us. Christ is willing to receive the poorest sinner in the world. He receives the lowest, the shabbiest, the vilest, the scum, the filth, the garbage of the world, for he is "lowly in heart." And out of such people as us, he builds a holy temple and gathers to himself trophies for his honor and praise. There are some great goldsmiths that can only think of preparing and polishing the choicest diamonds, but Jesus Christ polishes a common pebble and makes a jewel. Goldsmiths make their precious treasures out of precious materials; Christ makes his precious things out of rubbish.

If we wish to see the way of peace clearly, it is vital to understand that we must each come personally to Jesus for rest: "Come to me, all who labor." You must trust in him yourself. Jesus says, "Come to me"—not to anybody else but to "me." He does not say, *Come to hear a sermon about me* but "Come to me." He does not say, *Come to sacraments, which shall teach you something about me* but "Come to me"—to my work and person. Come to Jesus directly—to Jesus himself.

And here is his promise: "I will give you rest." This ought to be a very precious word to all believers. He promises to give you rest—be sure that you get it. Divest yourselves of your cares, your anxieties, your doubts, your fears. There he stands: he with the pierced feet and the nailed hands and the crimson side. There he stands in glory, and he bids you come to him and trust him—he is still gentle and lowly. Lay your burdens down at his feet. Why should you carry what he will readily carry for you? Tell him all your griefs. Why do you hide them from him? Should he not know your heart if you are married to him? Should there be a secret kept away from him? I am persuaded that I am pointing you to what will be more healing than the balm of Gilead and sweeter than the sweetest music to lull you into a delightful peace, if you will but listen to this gospel invitation and come to Jesus, by a simple act of faith and by a great resolve of fellowship, for he says, "I will give you rest."

REFLECT

Is this how you understand the heart of Jesus? What is it about his "gentle and lowly" heart that changes how you see him? What cares must you bring to him to deal gently with today so that you find rest for your soul?

PRAY

Spirit, teach me more about Christ's heart, disposition, character, and love towards me. Jesus, I want and need the rest you promise to all who come to you. Help me to relax into your heart. Revive me. I'm here, Lord. I bring you my burdens, ready for the rest you offer me, Jesus. Amen.

DAY 15

Jesus Feeds the Crowds

*Now when it was evening, the disciples came
to him and said, "This is a desolate place, and
the day is now over; send the crowds away to go
into the villages and buy food for themselves."
But Jesus said, "They need not go away; you
give them something to eat." They said to him,
"We have only five loaves here and two fish."
And he said, "Bring them here to me." Then
he ordered the crowds to sit down on the grass,
and taking the five loaves and the two fish, he
looked up to heaven and said a blessing. Then he
broke the loaves and gave them to the disciples,
and the disciples gave them to the crowds.
And they all ate and were satisfied. And they
took up twelve baskets full of the broken pieces
left over. And those who ate were about five
thousand men, besides women and children.*

MATTHEW 14:15-21

Look at the simple act of faith that Christ summons from his disciples: "Bring them here to me" (v 18). Let us bring all we have to Christ in faith, laying it at his feet, believing that his great power can make little means suffice for mighty ends.

Lord, there are only five loaves. They were only five loaves when we had them in our hands, but in his hands, they are food for five thousand men. *Lord, there are two fishes.* They were insignificant while they were ours, but his touch has ennobled them, and those little fishes have become food for a vast multitude. Blessed is the believer who, feeling that he or she has truly consecrated all to God, can say, "I do not want more talent. I do not need more affluence. I would not wish to have more—there is enough for my work and ministry. I know it is utterly insufficient in itself, but our sufficiency is of God." Oh, dear friends, we ought to believe that there are enough means when Christ blesses what we bring to him. We can bring our meager talents and abilities to him—and watch him work!

In bringing your talent to him, you put it into his hand, which was pierced for you. You give it to him who is your dearest friend. You give it to him who did not spare the blood of his heart, that he might redeem you. Do you not love him? Is it not an honor to be permitted to show your love to so notable and noble a person? When you have brought your talent to Christ, your next duty is to look up. Thank God for what you have got. Look up and say, "There is nothing in what I do. There is nothing in my prayers, my preachings, my goings, or my doings except your blessing. Lord, bless it!" He gives the blessing on it, and then he gives back to you to give to others. Meet with Christ on your own first; receive his blessing and bounty, and then serve others. We get in private what we distribute in public. He gives to us; we give to others. Do not discount the fish and bread in your hands. Do not doubt—Christ is with us, and we can. God is for us, and we are can. The Holy Ghost is in us, and we can. God the Holy Spirit calls us; Jesus Christ the Son of God cheers us; God the Father smiles upon us.

When the feast was finished, each disciple had a basketful of food to carry back to his Master's feet. Give yourself to Christ, and when you have used yourself for his glory, you will be more able to serve him than you are now. Think much of Christ. And consider how he can use you in his kingdom.

REFLECT

What is holding you back in serving others and sharing the gospel? What talents, abilities, and possessions of yours need to be put into the hands of Christ?

PRAY

Lord, you know what meager talents, skills, and gifts I possess. I bring them to you, awaiting your blessing, your power, and your sending of me out to serve and fill others with your blessing. Grow my faith, Lord. Overwhelm my excuses with the multiplying power of your grace. For your name. Amen.

DAY 16

Jesus Walks on Water

*But when the disciples saw him walking
on the sea, they were terrified, and said, "It
is a ghost!" and they cried out in fear. But
immediately Jesus spoke to them, saying,
"Take heart; it is I. Do not be afraid."*

MATTHEW 14:26-27

Some of the richest comforts are lost to us for lack of
clear perception. What could be a greater comfort
to the storm-tossed disciples than to know their Master
was present and to see him manifestly revealed as Lord
of sea as well as land? Yet because they did not discern
him clearly, they missed the incomparable comfort.
Christ walking on the wave should have put all fear to
rest, but instead they mistake him for a ghost appearing
amid the storm, bringing darker ill. But he utters the
great assurance, "It is I."

Oh, the excellence of faith which, like the telescope,
brings Christ near to us and lets us see him as he is! Oh,

the sweetness of walking near to Christ and knowing him with an assured, confident, clear knowledge that removes distresses which unnecessarily afflict us. What do you make of Christ?

We must know that Jesus is a real man who reigns above—he is no phantom, no ghost, no spirit but a risen man, touched with the feeling of our weaknesses, who pities us, loves us, and feels for us. And, in that capacity, he speaks to us out of the glory of heaven, and he says, "It is I; do not be afraid." Friend, be sure of the reality of the Christ you trust in. It is very easy to use the name of Jesus, but not quite so easy to know his person. It is common to talk about what he did and not to feel that he lives just as truly as we do, and that he is a person to be loved and to be trusted in just as much as our own brother or father or friend. We want a real, living, personal Christ! A phantom Christ will not cheer us in a storm. But a real Christ is a real consolation in a real storm. In whatever swirls about you today, hear him say, "It is I."

When our Lord says, "It is I," the Greek is literally rendered, "I am." Recall when God heard the cries of his ancient people enslaved in Egypt, and the Lord told Moses to comfort Israel by saying, "I AM has sent me to you" (Exodus 3:14). And when Jesus said, "I am" to his cowering disciples, they were drawn toward him, and yet they did not lose the awe of that incommunicable name "I AM." Then the disciples knew that Jesus was not only "I AM," but Immanuel—God with us. The "I AM" had come to their rescue and was in the ship with them. Here, dear friend, is your comfort and mine.

We will not fear the supernatural or the unseen, for we see Jesus, and in him we see the Father, and therefore we are of good cheer. Are your joys declining? Alas! It is a dying, fleeting world, but there is one who is always the same, for Jesus says to you, *I am; and because I live, you shall live also* (John 14:19). Be comforted; your Jesus still lives, for he says, *I AM*.

REFLECT

Meditate on the reality of Christ saying, "It is I." Are there any fears or concerns about which you need to hear Christ say, *I AM. Do not be afraid?*

PRAY

Jesus, I hear you say, "It is I." And I say, "It is *you*—my Savior, my Lord, my Redeemer, my Advocate, my Mediator, my Substitute, my Ransom, the Son of God, the Son of Man, my Friend." Grant me the great comfort and courage that can only come from hearing your words above the noise of the world, the flesh, and the devil. Amen.

DAY 17

Peter's Short Prayer

And Peter answered him, "Lord, if it is you,
command me to come to you on the water."
He said, "Come." So Peter got out of the boat
and walked on the water and came to Jesus.
But when he saw the wind, he was afraid, and
beginning to sink he cried out, "Lord, save me."

MATTHEW 14:28-33

As long as you have a heart to pray, God has an ear to hear. Look at Peter: he is "beginning to sink." The water is up to his knees; it is up to his waist; it is up to his neck; but it is not yet too late for him to cry, "Lord, save me." And he has no sooner said it than the hand of Jesus stretches out to catch him. So, Christian, cry to God, though the devil tells you it is no use. I cannot help feeling that Peter's short and simple prayer was uttered most naturally. Peter was in too great a peril to put any fine language into his prayer. He was too conscious of his danger; he just expressed the strong desire of his soul in the simplest manner possible: "Lord, save me." And that prayer was heard, and Peter was saved from drowning.

Where did Peter pray this prayer? It was not in a place set apart for public worship nor in his usual place for private prayer, but he prayed as he was sinking in the water. He was in great peril, so he cried out, "Lord, save me." It is good to assemble with God's people for prayer if you can, but if you cannot, it matters little, for prayer can ascend to him from anywhere, all over the world. It is good to have a special spot where you pray at home—at the same time, we must never allow ourselves to become the slaves of even such a good habit as that, and we must always remember that, if we really want to find the Lord by prayer, as one poet said:

> *Where'er we seek him, he is found,*
> *And every place is hallowed ground.*

Friends, it is good to have regular hours for devotion and to resort to the same place for prayer as far as possible, but still, the spirit of prayer is better even than the habit of prayer. It is better to be able to pray at all times than to make it a rule to pray at certain times and seasons. A Christian is more fully grown in grace when he or she prays about everything than they would if they only prayed under certain conditions and circumstances.

I always feel that there is something wrong if I go without prayer for even half an hour in the day. I cannot understand how a Christian can go from morning to evening without prayer. I cannot comprehend how they fight the battle of life without asking for the guardian care of God while the arrows of temptation are flying so thickly around them. I cannot imagine how they can decide what to do in times of perplexity, how they can see their own imperfections or the faults of others, without feeling constrained to say, all day long, "O Lord, guide me. O Lord, forgive me. O Lord, bless my friend!" I cannot think how they can be continually receiving mercies from the Lord without saying, "God be thanked for this new token of his grace!" Do not be content, dear brothers and sisters in Christ, unless you can pray everywhere and at all times and so obey the apostolic word, "Pray without ceasing" (1 Thessalonians 5:17).

Do you, dear friend, feel that you are not living as near to God as you once did? Is the chilling influence of the world telling upon you? Then pray, "Lord, save me." Have you fallen into some sin which you fear may bring disgrace upon your profession of faith? Well then, before that sin grows greater, cry, "Lord, save me." It may comfort the reader that although this was the prayer of a man in trouble, and a man in whom there was a mixture of unbelief and faith, it succeeded. Our imperfections and infirmities will not prevent prayer from speeding ahead, as long as it is sincere and earnest.

REFLECT

Are your prayers natural, honest, and sprinkled throughout the day? What simple request do you have for your Lord today?

PRAY

Offer a short and genuine prayer today. Start with, "Lord, help ___. End with "Lord, thank you for ___." And offer multiple short and simple prayers throughout the day.

DAY 18

Sit at Jesus' Feet

Now as they went on their way, Jesus entered a village. And a woman named Martha welcomed him into her house. And she had a sister called Mary, who sat at the Lord's feet and listened to his teaching. But Martha was distracted with much serving. And she went up to him and said, "Lord, do you not care that my sister has left me to serve alone? Tell her then to help me." But the Lord answered her, "Martha, Martha, you are anxious and troubled about many things, but one thing is necessary. Mary has chosen the good portion, which will not be taken away from her."

LUKE 10:38-42

The one thing necessary is what Mary chose—that good portion which should not be taken away from her. Very clearly this was to sit at Jesus' feet and hear his word. If anything is plain at all in holy Scripture, it is evident that this is the one thing we need: to sit at Jesus' feet and hear his word. This and nothing less: this and nothing more.

We are always to be learners and lovers of Jesus. Never let departure from him and independence of him be named among you. It is weakness, sickness, sin, and sorrow for a believer to leave the Lord and become either their own leader or reliance. We are only safe while we remain humbly and gladly ready to obey him. Jesus Christ is a monopolizer of human hearts; he will never accept just one part of our person. He bought us altogether, and he will have the whole of our personality. Christ must be everything, or he will be nothing. Christ must be first to us. We do not love Christ if we love anything as well as Christ. And neither do we trust Christ if we trust in anything besides. Christ must reign alone. "Jesus only" must be the motto of our spirits. It is good for us, therefore, that only one thing is necessary, for only one thing is possible. And from this one blessing flow many blessings.

To sit at Jesus' feet means holiness, for those who learn of Jesus learn no sin but are instructed in lovely things and things of good repute. It brings strength, for they who sit with Jesus and feed upon him are girded with his strength. It means zeal, for the love of Christ fires hearts that live upon it, and they that are much in the company of Jesus become like Jesus, so that the zeal of the Lord's house burns hot within them. So, when we say that sitting at Jesus' feet is the one thing necessary, we have not uttered a mere truism; it encompasses a world of blessings.

Christian, it is necessary for you today to have communion with Christ. Do not think of it as only indispensable tomorrow—it is needed now. There are dangers you cannot see which can only be warded off by present and immediate fellowship with Christ. "One thing is necessary." However much you advance, O believer, you never advance beyond this. Whatever your experience or your information or your ripeness for glory, it is still necessary to sit at Jesus' feet. You shall never get into a higher class in the school of wisdom than the class which Christ teaches. It is always necessary—every moment necessary—that we sit at Jesus' feet.

REFLECT

Is anything distracting you from sitting at Jesus' feet? What could you do to enjoy Christ's presence more?

PRAY:

Lord, help me to sit at your feet today, tomorrow, and all of my days. Communion with you is my greatest need, reward, and joy. Show me what is hindering me from unhurried fellowship with you. I'm ready to sit at your feet. In your name, Jesus. Amen.

DAY 19

The Good Shepherd

*I am the good shepherd. I know my own
and my own know me, just as the Father
knows me and I know the Father; and
I lay down my life for the sheep.*

JOHN 10:14-15

When our Lord says, "I am the good shepherd," he means to tell us that the real, the truest, the best, and the most sure example of shepherding is himself. Every good thing that you can imagine to be, or that should be, in a shepherd, you find in the Lord.

He is your owner and caretaker. The Lord Jesus Christ is never off duty. And he leads you, his sheep, wherever you have to go. Do you not see the blessed Shepherd leading your own pilgrimage? Can you not see him guiding your way? Let us respond, "Lead on, O blessed Lord; lead on, and we will follow the traces of your feet!"

Think on how he says, "I know my own and my own know me" (v 14). He knows our number. He will never lose one. He knows the number of those for whom he paid the ransom price. He knows the age and character of every one of his own. He assures us that the very hairs of our head are all numbered (Matthew 10:30). Christ doesn't have an unknown sheep. It is not possible that he should have overlooked or forgotten one of them. He has such an intimate knowledge of all who are redeemed with his most precious blood that he never mistakes one of them for another nor misjudges one of them. He knows our constitutions—those that are weak and feeble, those that are nervous and frightened, those that are strong, those that have a tendency to presumption, those that are sleepy, those that are brave, those that are sick, sorry, worried, or wounded. He knows those that are hunted by the devil, those that are caught up between the jaws of the lion and shaken till the very life is almost driven out of them. He knows our feelings, fears, and frights.

Our good Shepherd knows our sins. I often feel glad to think that he always did know our evil natures, and what would come of them. When he chose us, he knew what we were, and what we should be. He did not buy his sheep in the dark. He did not choose us without knowing all the devious ways of our past and future lives. Here is the splendor of his grace: "Whom he foreknew, he also predestined" (Romans 8:29). His election implies foreknowledge of all our ill manners. They say of human love that it is blind, but Christ's love has many eyes, and all its eyes are open, and yet he loves us still.

I like to think of our good Shepherd not merely as dying for us but as willingly laying down his life. When he spoke these words, it had not been done then. But now it has been done. "I lay down my life for the sheep" may now be read, *I have laid down my life for the sheep.* For you, beloved, he has given his hands to the nails and his feet to the cruel iron. For you he has borne the fever and the bloody sweat. For you he has cried "Eloi, Eloi, lema sabachthani" (Mark 15:34); for you he has given up the ghost. He glories in substitution for his people. He makes it his boast, when he speaks of his chosen, that he suffered in their stead: that he bore—that they might never bear—the wrath of God on account of sin. What he glories in, we also glory in. "But far be it from me to boast except in the cross of our Lord Jesus Christ, by which the world has been crucified to me, and I to the world" (Galatians 6:14). O beloved, what a blessed Christ we have, who loves us so, who knows us so— whom we also know and love!

REFLECT

How have you seen your Shepherd leading you this past year? Where do you need to follow his leading now?

PRAY

Only the good Shepherd, the Shepherd of shepherds, could know my fears, my sins, my failings, my doubts, and my weaknesses and love me still. Thank you, Jesus. I look to you again today, my Shepherd. Lead me to your green pasture. I will lack no good thing with you, my Lord. Amen.

DAY 20

Only Jesus

*And after six days Jesus took with him Peter
and James, and John his brother, and led them
up a high mountain by themselves. And he was
transfigured before them, and his face shone like
the sun, and his clothes became white as light.*

*And behold, there appeared to them Moses and
Elijah, talking with him. And Peter said to Jesus,
"Lord, it is good that we are here. If you wish, I
will make three tents here, one for you and one for
Moses and one for Elijah." He was still speaking
when, behold, a bright cloud overshadowed
them, and a voice from the cloud said, "This is
my beloved Son, with whom I am well pleased;
listen to him." When the disciples heard this,
they fell on their faces and were terrified. But
Jesus came and touched them, saying, "Rise,
and have no fear." And when they lifted up
their eyes, they saw no one but Jesus only.*

MATTHEW 17:1-8

When Peter saw our Lord with Moses and Elijah, he exclaimed, "Lord, it is good that we are here," as if he was implying that it was better to be with Jesus and Moses and Elijah than to be with Jesus only. Now, it was certainly good that once in his life he should see Christ transfigured with the representatives of the Law and the Prophets. But depend on it, brothers and sisters, that ravishing and exciting experiences, though they may be useful as occasional refreshments, are not so good for every day as that quiet but delightful ordinary fellowship with "Jesus only" (v 8)—which ought to be the distinguishing mark of every Christian life.

I desire, for my fellow Christians and for myself, that more and more the great object of our thoughts, motives, and acts may be "Jesus only." I believe that whenever our religion is most lively, it is most full of Christ. Moreover, when it is most practical, absolute, and common sense, it always gets nearest to Jesus. I can bear witness that whenever I am in deep sorrow, nothing will do for me but "Jesus only." I retreat to the innermost citadel of our holy faith—namely, to the very heart of Christ—when my spirit is assailed by temptation or gripped with anguish. What is more, my witness is that whenever I have high spiritual enjoyments—rich, rare, celestial—they are always connected with "Jesus only." Other religious things may give some kind of joy, and joy that is healthy too, but the sublimest, the most inebriating, the most divine of all joys must be found in "Jesus only."

For "Jesus only" shall be our reward; to be with him where he is, to behold his glory, to be like him when we shall see him as he is—we ask no other heaven. Our souls can conceive of no other bliss. May the Lord grant that we have a fullness of this and that "Jesus only" shall be our delight throughout eternity. I find if I want to labor much, I must live on Jesus only. If I desire to suffer patiently, I must feed on Jesus only. If I wish to wrestle with God successfully, I must plead Jesus only. If I aspire to conquer sin, I must use the blood of Jesus only. If I long to learn the mysteries of heaven, I must seek the teachings of Jesus only.

I believe that anything which we add to Christ lowers our position: that the more elevated our soul becomes—the closer to what it will be when it shall enter the region of the perfect—the more completely everything else will sink and die out; and Jesus, Jesus, Jesus only will be first and last, the Alpha and Omega of every thought of our heads and pulse of our hearts. May it be so with every Christian!

REFLECT

Is there anything in your life or relationship with God that you are hoping for or relying on in addition to "Jesus only"? What do you think would need to change for all your hope to be found in Jesus alone?

PRAY

Lord, if I were there on the mountain top, I am sure I would have responded just like Peter or worse. Help me not to be more impressed and attentive to others than to you. You are the only reason why I was saved. Empower me, Spirit, to live for Jesus only. Amen.

DAY 21

Bring It to Jesus

And when they came to the crowd, a man came up to him and, kneeling before him, said, "Lord, have mercy on my son, for he has seizures and he suffers terribly. For often he falls into the fire, and often into the water. And I brought him to your disciples, and they could not heal him." And Jesus answered, "O faithless and twisted generation, how long am I to be with you? How long am I to bear with you? Bring him here to me." And Jesus rebuked the demon, and it came out of him, and the boy was healed instantly.

MATTHEW 17:14-18

The kingdom of our Lord Jesus Christ, while on earth, was so extensive as to touch the confines of both heaven and hell. We see him at one moment discoursing with Moses and Elijah in his glory, as though at heaven's gates, and then—after a few hours—we see him confronting a foul spirit, as though defying the infernal pit. There is a long journey from patriarchs to demons, from prophets to dumb devils; yet mercy prompts him and power supports him so that he is equally glorious in either place. What a glorious Lord he was, even while in his humiliation! How glorious is he now! How far his goodness reaches! Truly he has dominion from sea to sea; his empire reaches to the extremes of the human condition. Our Lord's transfiguration did not disqualify him for casting out the devils; neither did it make him too superior and spiritual to grapple with human ills, and so, even now, the glories of heaven do not take him away from the miseries of earth, nor do they make him forget the cries of the feeble ones who are seeking him in this valley of tears.

There is no demon, however forceful, who will not tremble if Jesus speaks or even so much as looks at him. Today, Jesus is the Master of hearts and consciences, and by his secret power, he can work upon every one of our minds. There cannot be a case that is too hard for him; we only need to bring it to him. I know we are tempted to think of him as of one far away who does not behold the sorrows of his church, but, I tell you, Christ's honor is as much concerned at this moment with the defeat or victory of his servants as it was when he came down from the mountain top. He is ready for his brothers and sisters to bring him their needs.

The highest sin and the deepest despair together cannot baffle the power of Jesus. If you were between the very jaws of hell, Christ could snatch you out. If your sins had brought you even to the gates of hell, so that the flames flashed into your face, if then you looked to Jesus, he could save you. If you are brought to him when you are at death's door, yet still eternal mercy will receive you. Christ unable to save? Never. Christ outdone by Satan and by sin? Impossible. A sinner with diseases too many for the great Physician to heal? I tell you that if all the diseases and all the sins of men were heaped on you, and blasphemy and murder and fornication and adultery and every sin that is possible or imaginable had all been committed by you, yet the precious blood of Jesus Christ, God's dear Son, cleanses us from all sin. Where Jesus heals, he heals forever. Once he brings the soul out of prison, it will not go back again. If he says, *I forgive*, the sin is forgiven; if he speaks peace, the peace shall be like a river that never ceases, running until it pours away into the ocean of eternal love.

REFLECT

Today, do you have any doubts about Jesus' care and concern for you? What temptations, distresses, or sorrows do you need to bring to him?

PRAY

Use this time to bring your need to Christ.

DAY 22

Christ, Greater Than Solomon

Behold, something greater than Solomon is here.

LUKE 11:31

Our first thought is that no mere man would have said this about himself unless he had been altogether eaten up with vanity. For among the Jews, Solomon was the very ideal of greatness and wisdom. It would be an instance of the utmost self-conceit if any mere man were to say of himself, "Something greater than Solomon is here." But we know that Christ is no mere man.

Christ knows who he is and what he is, and he is not lowly in spirit because he is ignorant of his own greatness. He was meek and lowly in heart—*servus servorum,* as the Latins were prone to call him: Servant of servants. But all the while he knew that he was *Rex regum,* or King of kings. He takes a towel, and he washes his disciples' feet, but all the while he knows that he is their Master and their Lord. He associates with tax collectors and harlots, and dwells with the common people, but all the while he knows that he is the only begotten of the

Father. He wears a peasant's garb and has nowhere to lay his head, but he knows that whatever the lowliness of his condition, he is greater than Solomon. It is grand humility on Christ's part that he lowers himself to be our servant—our Savior—when he is so great that the greatest of men are as nothing before him.

In his nature, the Lord Jesus is greater than Solomon. Alas, poor Solomon! How different is our Lord! There is no sin in Christ—no folly in the incarnate God. The backsliding of Solomon finds no parallel in Jesus, in whom the prince of this world found nothing to dishonor—though he searched him through and through. Our Lord is greater than Solomon because he is not mere man. He is perfect man—man to the utmost of humanity, minus sin. But still, he is more, and infinitely more, than man. "For in him the whole fullness of deity dwells bodily" (Colossians 2:9). He is God himself; "The Word was God" (John 1:1). God dwells in him, and he himself is God. Look at the real greatness of character in both Christ and Solomon for a minute, and you can hardly see Solomon with a microscope, while Christ rises grandly before you, growing every moment till he fills the whole horizon of your admiration.

Let us go about our day with this resolve in our minds: that we will speak more highly of Christ than we have done; that we will try to love him more and serve him better and make him, in our own estimation and in the world's, greater than he has ever been. Oh, for a glorious high throne to set him on and a crown of stars to place upon his head! Oh, to bring nations to his feet! I know my words cannot honor him according to his merits. I am quite sure to fail in my own judgment when telling out his excellence. He is too glorious for my feeble language to describe. If I could speak with the tongues of men and of angels, I could not speak worthily of him. If I could borrow all the harmonies of heaven and enlist every harp and song of the glorified, the music would not be sweet enough for his praises. Our glorious Redeemer is ever blessed—let us bless him. He is to be extolled above the highest heavens—let us sound forth his praises.

O my brothers and sisters, sound out the praises of Jesus Christ! Sound out that precious name! There is none like it under heaven to stir my heart. I hope you can all say the same. I know you can, if you love him, for all renewed hearts are enamored of the sweet Lord Jesus. One "greater than Solomon is here." Solomon has no power over your hearts, but Jesus does. His influence is infinitely greater. His power to bless is infinitely greater, and so let us magnify and adore him with all our hearts.

REFLECT

Praise Jesus for all the ways that he is greater than Solomon.

PRAY

King Jesus, you are so much greater than Solomon. You are a greater sage, a greater King, a greater leader, a greater lover of our souls. Only you, the sinless Son of David, can save me from my sins. Thank you, Jesus. Amen.

DAY 23

The Cost of Discipleship

*For which of you, desiring to build a tower, does
not first sit down and count the cost, whether he
has enough to complete it? Otherwise, when he
has laid a foundation and is not able to finish,
all who see it begin to mock him, saying, "This
man began to build and was not able to finish."
... So therefore, any one of you who does not
renounce all that he has cannot be my disciple.*

LUKE 14:28-30, 33

True religion is costly. Now, the gifts of God's grace
cost us nothing; neither could his salvation be purchased with money nor with merit nor by vows and
penances. The gospel motto is "Without money and
without price" (Isaiah 55:1). We are "justified by his
grace as a gift, through the redemption that is in Christ
Jesus" (Romans 3:24). Yet, for all that, if anyone will be
Christ's disciple, it will cost them something. There are
costs to count: when my own pleasure or my own gain

or my own reputation or even my own life shall come in the way of Christ's glory, I shall count all things as rubbish and loss for the surpassing worth of knowing Christ Jesus our Lord (Philippians 3:8).

If we see anything in ourselves opposed to Jesus, we must do away with it. We must kill the flesh with its affections and lusts, denying anything and everything which would grieve the Savior or would prevent our becoming conformed to him. We must make an unreserved surrender of all to Jesus. Listen to these words: "Any one of you who does not renounce all that he has cannot be my disciple" (Luke 14:33). No one has truly given himself or herself to the Lord Jesus Christ unless they have also said, "My Lord, I give to you this day my body, my soul, my powers, my talents, my goods, my house, my children, and all that I have. I have surrendered all to you."

You cannot be Christ's disciple at any less expense than this; if you possess a penny that is your own and not your Master's, Christ is not your Master. It must all be his, every single jot, or you cannot be his. If you must give up any pleasure, it is because it is not a fitting pleasure for you—it is poisonous sugar of lead (an archaic sweetener derived from lead) and not true sweetness. Christ will give you greater enjoyments by far. Are you willing? Then the Spirit of God will help you. You shall give up the world and the flesh without a sigh. You shall fight against your lusts, and you shall overcome them through the blood of the Lamb. The tower shall be built, and the Lord shall inhabit it. Cast yourselves on Jesus by a simple faith; rest in his power and from day to day believe in his strength, and he will bear you safely through.

Remember that our Redeemer does not ask us to do what he has not done himself. That thought pierces me to the quick—I hope it will affect you also. "Lord, do you bid me to leave my father's house if it must be for your sake?" Didn't he leave the glorious mansions of heaven? "What if I am called to bear reproach?" They called our Master "Beelzebub." "What if I get cast out by others?" They also cast out Jesus. When we think of the scourging, the shame, and the spitting which our Lord endured, what are our griefs? And if, for his sake, we should even be condemned to death, we know how he hung on the cross, stripped of his all, that he might save us from the wrath to come. O believer, can you follow your Lord wherever he goes? Soldiers of the cross, can you follow him? There he is in the center of the battle, where the attacks fall fastest—will you follow him? Dare you follow him, or do you long for the tents of ease and the soft couches of the cowards who are shrinking back and deserting to the enemy? Count the cost, remember the price, and go forward with him.

REFLECT

What costs of discipleships have you not added to the list of loss for the sake of following Christ? Does anything need to be surrendered today?

PRAY

Lord, help me value the right things. Keep me from mis-counting. May I never cut corners, fudge the numbers, or cook the books of discipleship with you. Help me count the cost of being crucified and raised with you, my Lord Jesus. Amen.

DAY 24

The Prodigal Son

And he arose and came to his father. But while he was still a long way off, his father saw him and felt compassion, and ran and embraced him and kissed him. And the son said to him, "Father, I have sinned against heaven and before you. I am no longer worthy to be called your son." But the father said to his servants, "Bring quickly the best robe, and put it on him, and put a ring on his hand, and shoes on his feet. And bring the fattened calf and kill it, and let us eat and celebrate. For this my son was dead, and is alive again; he was lost, and is found." And they began to celebrate.

LUKE 15:20-24

Let's see what our Lord wants to teach us about God's heart by his parable of the prodigal son.

The father "saw" his son (v 20). There is a great deal in that word "saw." He saw who it was, saw where he had come from, saw the pig-worker's clothes, saw the filth upon his hands and feet, saw his rags, saw his repentant look, saw what he had been, saw what he was, and saw what he would soon be. Friends, God has a way of seeing men and women that you and I cannot understand. He sees right through us at a glance, as if we were made of glass. He sees all our past, present, and future. "But while he was still a long way off, his father saw him" (v 20). It was not with icy eyes that the father looked on his returning son. He saw a sinner long before the sinner saw him.

We see that the prodigal's father ran. Slow are the steps of repentance, but swift are the feet of forgiveness. God can run when we can scarcely limp, and if we are limping towards him, he will run towards us. Dear reader, God has compassion on the woes and miseries of us sinners. We may have brought our troubles on ourselves, but nevertheless God has compassion upon us. The compassion of God is followed by swift movements. He is slow to anger, but he is quick to bless. He does not take any time to consider how he shall show his love to returning prodigals—that was all done in the eternal covenant. He has no need to prepare for their return to him—that was all done on Calvary. God comes flying in the greatness of his compassion to help every poor, penitent soul.

Notice how the father "embraced him and kissed him." The kindliness of God towards repentant sinners is very great. He seems to stoop from his throne of glory to embrace a repentant sinner. God embracing a sinner! What a wonderful picture! Can you imagine it? When God's arm is about our neck and his lips are on our cheek, kissing us much, then we understand more than preachers or books can ever tell us of his loving kindness.

And then the father graced his son with new clothes. There was the robe—the dress of a son, and of a son who was beloved and accepted. Have you noticed how the son's confession was met with the robe? The sentences match each other thus: "Father, I have sinned … Bring quickly the best robe and put it on him." And so the Father covers all our sins with Christ's righteousness. He puts away our sin by crediting to us the righteousness of Jesus.

As the festival was about to begin, the prodigal needed a fitting and festive garment. It would not have been right for him to feast and be merry in those rags. The father put the best robe on him that he would be ready to take his place at the banquet. So, when the repentant sinner comes to God, his or her past is not only covered by the righteousness of Christ, but they are prepared for the future blessedness which is reserved for the pardoned ones, and then they are fitted to begin the rejoicing at once.

REFLECT

What aspects of God's heart resonate with your soul today? Is anything keeping you from enjoying your robes of Christ's righteousness?

PRAY

God, you took away my rags and gave me the righteousness of the Son. I was longing for pig food, and then you set me at your table. What a merciful and loving God! Thank you Jesus. Amen.

DAY 25

To Seek and Save the Lost

For the Son of Man came to
seek and to save the lost.

LUKE 19:10

O fellow sinner, is it not pure joy to know that the Son of God has come in the humble title of the Son of Man to save us? He is no stern son of Zeus or a Roman god with a severe countenance and blood-thirsty commands. He is Jesus, the "man of sorrows and acquainted with grief" (Isaiah 53:3). It is as your brother, touched with a feeling of your infirmities, that Jesus comes to you. He has, moreover, come in a mediatorial capacity, for "there is one mediator between God and men, the man Christ Jesus" (1 Timothy 2:5). He can put his hand upon you and, at the same time, lay his hand upon the Father. He who bridges the gulf between the misery of fallen humanity and the eternal dignity of the unsullied God has come to save the lost.

We know that all people are lost in Adam. As soon

as we are born into this world, we are lost. "Behold," says David, "I was brought forth in iniquity, and in sin did my mother conceive me" (Psalm 51:5); "In Adam all die" (1 Corinthians 15:22). The fall of Adam was the fall of the human race. My dear friends, you and I were lost in the sense of having broken the law of God, but Jesus came and took our sin upon himself and bore the wrath of God as our assurance and our substitute so that God can now be the just and yet the justifier of all who believe in Jesus (Romans 3:26). Christ literally took upon himself the transgression and iniquity of his people and was made a curse for us, seeing that we had fallen under the wrath of God. Christ seeks and saves the lost from sin and all its consequences by his most precious death and resurrection.

First, we see that Christ saved us from the power of Satan. The seed of the woman has bruised the serpent's head, so that Satan's power is broken (Genesis 3:15). Next, he also saves us from the guilt of past sin. In one moment, as soon as the blood of Christ is applied to the conscience, every past sin is gone, and in God's sight, it is as if we had never sinned. The next thing he does is kill the power of sin within and makes us believers new creatures. And do not forget this precious truth of the gospel—Christ saves us from future falling. He saves, not only for a year or for ten years and then lets people go—no, he finally and completely saves that which was lost. We do not preach that Christ forgives sinners and then lets them live as before. No, the moment he gives pardon of sin, he gives a new nature too. The gospel hospital is not merely a place where lepers are harbored but where lepers are healed.

I shall never forget how he found me—how he first gained my ear and then my desires, so that I wished to have him for my Lord, and then he taught me to trust him. And when I had trusted him and found that I was saved, then I loved him—and I love him still. I hope that among those who read these pages, there will be many whom the Lord Jesus has specially redeemed with his most precious blood, and I trust that he will appear at once to them and say to each one of them, "I have loved you with an everlasting love; therefore I have continued my faithfulness to you" (Jeremiah 31:3).

REFLECT
Have you been found by the Lord Jesus? Look to him and his work for you and trust him to save you. If you have been saved by Jesus, how are you enjoying the freedom and comforts he's purchased for you?

PRAY
Son of Man, I remember this Easter season how you seek and save the lost. I was lost in unbelief, turned around in sin, and deceived by the directions of the devil until the beacon of the gospel brought me home to you. Bring more lost sinners home, Holy Spirit! In your name, Son of Man. Amen.

DAY 26

Face Like Flint

I gave my back to those who strike,
and my cheeks to those who pull out the beard;
I hid not my face from disgrace and spitting.
But the Lord GOD helps me;
therefore I have not been disgraced;
therefore I have set my face like a flint,
and I know that I shall not be put to shame.

ISAIAH 50:6-7

These are, in prophecy, the words of the Messiah. This is the language of Christ Jesus, the promised Deliverer, whom God sent into the world to be the one and only Savior. This is the declaration of Jesus of Nazareth, the King of the Jews—it is he who said in prophecy, "I have set my face like a flint" and afterwards carried it out in actual life.

Luke seems to have had this passage in his mind when he wrote about our Lord, "When the days drew near for him to be taken up, he set his face to go to Jerusalem"

(Luke 9:51). There is the same meaning in the two passages, and I cannot help feeling that the words recorded by Isaiah were brought to the memory of Luke by the Holy Spirit when he penned that expression. The fact is that our Master, even from eternity, resolved to save his people, and nothing could keep him from the accomplishment of his purpose.

From eternity, he foresaw that we would fall from our first estate, and he entered into covenant engagements to redeem us. And from the pledge he gave of old, he never pulled back. Time rolled on, and humanity fell and afterwards multiplied upon the face of the earth, but Christ's delights were still with the human race. Often, in one form or another, he would visit this earth to converse with Abraham or to wrestle with Jacob or to speak with Joshua or to walk in the burning fiery furnace with Shadrach, Meshach, and Abednego. He was always anticipating the time when he should actually assume human nature and fulfill his covenant engagements.

At last, the appointed hour arrived, and then he did not disdain the virgin's womb or the Bethlehem manger or the workshop of Nazareth. Even as a child, he said, "Did you not know that I must be in my Father's house?" (Luke 2:49). The set purpose of redeeming his people was an all-consuming passion that ever burned within his soul. For what he once said to his disciples, he felt always: "I have a baptism to be baptized with, and how great is my distress until it is accomplished!" (12:50). He felt bound and hampered until he could get to his chief work—he longed to be at it. With wholehearted passion, he desired to eat that last Passover meal on the eve of himself becoming God's Passover Lamb.

Reflect on this passage in the letter to the Hebrews: "… who for the joy that was set before him endured the cross, despising the shame" (Hebrews 12:2). His joys were many: 1) the joy of saving immortal souls; 2) the joy of vindicating the broken law of God; 3) the joy of breaking down the power of evil in the world and setting up a kingdom of goodness and of love; 4) the joy of bringing a remedy for all humanity's diseases—a cure-all for their miseries; 5) the joy of gathering unto himself a multitude that no one can number—redeemed by blood out of every nation and family and tongue, who should glorify God for ever and ever.

We serve a Master who steadfastly set his face to go to Jerusalem in order that he might accomplish the one great purpose for which he came to earth and from which he could not be turned. Therefore, we ought to be faithful to him and to partake as far as we can of his spirit. Does he not seem to rebuke us without saying a word—for his face was set like a flint, while our faces often blush with shame when we are called upon to speak up for him, or perhaps when we are too ashamed to do so? If we truly follow such a Lord as Christ is, we also ought to be flinty-faced for all holy purposes, and I ask you, dear friends, to pray to God the Holy Spirit to make you so.

REFLECT

How does Christ's resolve to save you affect your mindset about being his witness? Where do you need to find a flinty face in your walk and mission with Christ?

PRAY

Lord, nothing and no one could stop you from accomplishing the salvation of sinners. The devil tried, the disciples tried, and even those hanging next to you at Golgotha tried to stop you from dying on the cross. Praise you, Lord. Thank you, Lord. Help me to keep my eyes on you as I run my race with endurance. For your name's sake. Amen.

DAY 27

Jesus Rides into Jerusalem

They brought the donkey and the colt and put on them their cloaks, and he sat on them. Most of the crowd spread their cloaks on the road, and others cut branches from the trees and spread them on the road. And the crowds that went before him and that followed him were shouting, "Hosanna to the Son of David! Blessed is he who comes in the name of the Lord! Hosanna in the highest!" And when he entered Jerusalem, the whole city was stirred up, saying, "Who is this?" And the crowds said, "This is the prophet Jesus, from Nazareth of Galilee."

MATTHEW 21:7–11

Why ride into Jerusalem in this form and fashion? Let me share two out of many reasons for our Lord's humble ride.

First, that he might most openly declare himself as King. He had told them who he was and why he came, but they would not hear it, and they dared say to him, "If you are the Christ, tell us plainly" (John 10:24).

Now he will assure them still more positively of his kingdom by openly riding into the city of Jerusalem. Second, it was our Lord's public claiming of authority over Israel, as promised by the prophets. He was the Son of David, and, moreover, as the Messiah, the King of his people, ancient Israel. The prophet said, concerning him, "Rejoice greatly, O daughter of Zion! Shout aloud, O daughter of Jerusalem! Behold, your king is coming to you; righteous and having salvation is he, humble and mounted on a donkey, on a colt, the foal of a donkey" (Zechariah 9:9). Our Lord Jesus literally came to Zion in this manner—and he put the city in a stir.

Jesus Christ never moved the people of Jerusalem till he rode that donkey—till they cast their garments in the road and strewed the branches and cried, "Hosanna!" Only then, as he rode in triumph as King of the Jews, was the whole city stirred. Oh, that we had a reigning Savior more distinctly recognized in all our churches! And is your heart stirred when you think of Christ riding toward you?

Look! Here comes the King of the kings of the earth, not on a majestic steed—no prancing horse which would keep the sons in poverty at a distance. No, he rides upon his donkey and, as he rides along, speaks kindly to the little children, who are crying, "Hosanna," and wishes well to the mothers and fathers of the lowest society, who crowd around him. Christ is approachable. He is not divided from us. No trumpet sounds—he is content with the voice of men. No pomp but the pomp which loving hearts willingly yield to him. He rides toward the arrest, the trial, the nails, the cross, the mockery, and the horror, all for you. Brothers and sisters, may we belong to this way of the kingdom too. May we feel in our hearts that Christ has arrived and cast down every high and every proud thought—that every valley may be lifted up, and every hill may be brought low, and the whole heart exalted in that day as we say, "Hosanna!"

The best interpretation I can give of "Hosanna" is "Save, oh, save! Save, oh, save!" Different nations have different ways of expressing their goodwill to their monarchs. A Roman would have shouted, *"Io triumphe!"* The Brits sing, "God save the King." The Persians said, "O King, live forever." The French have their *"Vive"* expressions, by which they mean, "Long live…" "Hosanna" is tantamount to all these. It is a shout of homage, welcome, and loyalty. *Hosanna, Hosanna, the King is come. Save him, O Lord! Save us through him! Long live the King!* While it was a shout of reverence, it was also a prayer to the King, and we join in and say, "Save, Lord; save us, O King! O King, born to conquer and to save, deliver us!"

REFLECT

When was your heart last stirred by the glory of Christ? Are your affections and adoration warmed and awakened by his mighty acts of love and mercy to save you?

PRAY

All hail King Jesus! Hosanna! Hosanna! It is a sweet
song upon my lips to say with all of the redeemed,
"Hosanna!" I heartily say to the King of kings, "Long
live the King!" And as the risen King, your reign will
have no end. Hosanna! Blessed are you, my God and
King! Amen!

DAY 28

Jerusalem, Jerusalem

*O Jerusalem, Jerusalem, the city that kills
the prophets and stones those who are sent
to it! How often would I have gathered your
children together as a hen gathers her brood
under her wings, and you were not willing!*

MATTHEW 23:37

It is a marvelous thing that God should stoop to be compared to a hen: that Christ—the Son of the Highest, the Savior—should stoop to so lowly a piece of imagery as to liken himself to a hen. There must be something very instructive in this metaphor, or our Lord would not have used it.

Have you noticed how a hen is like a cover of safety to her little chicks? There is a hawk in the sky; the mother bird can see it, though the baby chickens cannot. She gives her particular cluck of warning, and quickly they come and hide beneath her wings. The hawk will not hurt them now, for under her wings they are secure.

This is what God is to those who come to him by Jesus Christ—he is the giver of safety. "He will cover you with his feathers; you will take refuge under his wings. His faithfulness will be a protective shield" (Psalm 91:4, CSB). When we run to Christ and hide under him, we shall be preserved from the attraction of our old sins or the danger of future temptations.

The hen is the source of comfort to her chicks. It is a cold night, and they would be frozen if they remained outside, but she calls them in, and when they are under her wings, they derive warmth from their mother. She will sit so carefully and keep her wings so widely spread that they may all be housed. What a cabin—what a palace it is for the young chicks to shelter there under the mother's wings! The snow may fall, or the rain may come pelting down, but the wings of the hen cocoon the chicks. And you, dear friend, if you run to Christ, will not only have safety but comfort. There is a deep, sweet comfort from hiding yourself away in God. For when troubles come, wave upon wave, blessed is the one who has a God to give them mercy upon mercy. Whether that is affliction, suffering, loss of property, or sickness, there is nothing needed but your God. Ten thousand things, apart from him, cannot satisfy you or give you comfort. If you hide away under his wings, you are as happy in him as the chicks are beneath the hen.

The hen is also the fountain of love to her chicks. Have you ever seen a hen fight for her chicks? She is a timid enough creature at any other time, but there is no timidity when her chicks are in danger. What an affection she has for them! But, oh, if you want to know the true fountain of love, you must run to Christ! The love of Jesus displayed at the cross and maintained from the throne can bring our hearts to overflowing.

Christ gathers us under his wings by making himself known to us. When we come to understand who he is and what he is and know something of his love—his tenderness and greatness—then we come to him. Ignorance keeps us away from him. But to know God and his Son, Jesus Christ, is eternal life (John 17:3). So, I urge you to study the Scriptures diligently and, as often as you can, to hear the gospel faithfully preached so that, knowing the Lord, you may be drawn towards him by that knowledge. These are the cords of love with which the Spirit of God draws us to Christ. He makes Christ known to us, and he shows us Christ in the wonder of his divine and human nature—Christ in the humiliation of his sufferings, Christ in the glory of his resurrection, Christ in the love of his heart, in the power of his arm, in the power of his petition, in the virtue of his blood—and, as we learn these sacred lessons, we say, "That is the Christ for me. That is the God for me," and we are gathered to him.

REFLECT

Is there anything keeping you from running to Christ—is it the very thing that should cause you to run toward him? Go to him for comfort, safety, and the soothing warmth of his love.

PRAY

Lord, you are the comfort I need. The safety my soul seeks is found under your wings of grace and peace. May I find no other home than your presence. Quiet my spirit with the sovereign protection you give to your loved ones. No snake, fox, or wolf can harm me. Nuzzle me near your heart, Lord Jesus. Amen.

DAY 29

Anointed and Adored

*Six days before the Passover, Jesus therefore came
to Bethany, where Lazarus was, whom Jesus
had raised from the dead. So they gave a dinner
for him there. Martha served, and Lazarus was
one of those reclining with him at table. Mary
therefore took a pound of expensive ointment
made from pure nard, and anointed the feet of
Jesus and wiped his feet with her hair. The house
was filled with the fragrance of the perfume.*

JOHN 12:1-3

Mary's deed came from a soul all on fire—the deed
of a woman filled with deep devotion and rever-
ent love. Deep thought led to burning love, and burning
love led to immediate action. Beloved friends, Christ's
church needs a band of men and women full of enthusiasm, who will go beyond others in devotion to the Lord
Jesus. We need missionaries who will dare to die to carry the gospel to regions beyond. We need ministers who

will defy public opinion and with flaming zeal burn a way into people's hearts. We need men and women who will consecrate all that they have by daring deeds of heroic sacrifice. Oh, that all Christians were like this! Where are we to get them? How are they to be produced?

The Holy Spirit's way to train men and women who will greatly serve Christ is to lead them to deep thought and quiet contemplation. There they obtain the knowledge and vital principles which are the fuel of true zeal. You cannot leap into great devotion; neither can you be preached into it nor dream yourself into it nor be electrified into it by revivalism. It must, through the divine energy of the Holy Spirit, arise out of watchful dealing with your soul and the near and dear communion with your Savior. You must sit at his feet, or you will never anoint them. He must pour his divine teaching into you, or you will never pour out precious ointment upon him. Mary is a great model of spiritual service for Christ.

As Mary brought all of the costly perfume to Jesus, she poured all of it upon him. She didn't fear judgment from Judas—this was all for Jesus. I do not think she gave a thought to Martha or to Lazarus or to any of them. The whole pound (450g) was for Jesus. The highest way of living is to live for Jesus and altogether for Jesus—not caring what another says or judges but feeling that, as Christ has bought us with his blood, we are his from the crown of our head to the sole of our foot, and we therefore have no master but our Redeemer. Consecrate to the Savior all that you have: every faculty, power, possession, and ability. Half the pound (225g) of pure nard would not have sufficed. That half-pound in reserve would have spoiled the deed. Perhaps we should never have heard of Mary's act at all if it had been less complete. Half a heart given to Christ? Never. Half a life given to Christ? Half your faculties, half your powers given to Christ? It is an unworthy gift. He gave you his all, and he claims all of you.

Brothers and sisters, do you live for Jesus in this way? Do we not perform many actions under the impulse of secondary motives? For my part, I like sometimes to do an act of which I feel "I am doing it alone for Jesus. Whether a soul shall be saved or not is not my main care, but I am speaking this good word in his honor. And if God accepts it and it glorifies Jesus, my end is served." Oh, it is a blessed thing to feel that you are living not as a servant of man nor of the church nor of a sect or party but for him whose precious blood has bought you! O dear soul, if you wish to fill the house with sweet odor, bring your whole self and pour out your heart at his feet!

REFLECT

Are you holding back any part of yourself from Christ? Are you tangled in mixed motives? What are you wanting and waiting to do for Christ—to pour out for him?

PRAY

Lord, teach me to live all for you. May my love for you grow to such a degree that I readily pour my heart, money, time, passions, and skills all at your feet. It is no sacrifice to surrender all to my Savior. Unclog my heart so I can give it all to you, Jesus. Amen.

DAY 30

Jesus Washes Feet

*Jesus, knowing that the Father had given all
things into his hands, and that he had come
from God and was going back to God, rose
from supper. He laid aside his outer garments,
and taking a towel, tied it around his waist.
Then he poured water into a basin and began
to wash the disciples' feet and to wipe them with
the towel that was wrapped around him.*

JOHN 13:3-5

I f you look through this chapter, you do not find that
Peter asked Christ to wash his feet. It was unsolicited
and unexpected. Christ comes, without any prayers or
supplications from the disciples, and he begins to wash
their feet. It is great goodness on Christ's part to hear
our prayers when we really feel our need—but does he
perform for us such menial, such generous acts as to
wash our feet without being asked? O beloved, if Christ
only did for us what we ask him to do we should perish

forever, for nine out of ten of the things which he gives us we never asked for. We do not know our own needs. The Lord Jesus so loves his people that every day he is washing our feet.

Jesus has washed all believers, once for all, in his most precious blood. Before the bar of justice, cleansing is completely accomplished forever for all the chosen, by the great bloodshed upon Calvary. That is a matter of the past—a thing for which to bless God for all eternity. But here is another kind of washing—not of the entire body but of the feet only and not with blood but with water. Does our Lord Jesus do anything of this kind now—anything so humbling to himself and yet so needed by us? I answer, yes, he does.

The Savior performs a parallel action when he watches over the temporal affairs of his people. You know, beloved, that not a hair of your head falls to the ground without his care. Your most trifling trouble may be taken in prayer to Christ, for Jesus waits to be gracious to his own beloved. Now, when Jesus superintends our ordinary comings and goings, looks to our family troubles, and bears our household cares, saying to us, *Cast all your care on me, for I care for you* (1 Peter 5:7), is he not, in effect, doing for us what he did for Peter? Washing our feet and caring for our lowest parts and minding our poor dust-stained feet?

Consider further how he cares for our minor matters with a personal interest. That Christ should ease the disciples' weary hearts I can understand, or, that he should enlighten their clouded brains I can understand. But that he should wash their feet is wonderful. A little soil on their ankles—will he attend to that? He will, and personally too. He will take the basin and the towel himself and wash their feet. Had they been diseased with leprosy or been blind, it would have made sense that he would heal them. But a mere defilement of their feet is so small a matter; would he attend to that? He might have left them to wash one another's feet, might he not? But, no, the Lord laid aside his own garments and took a towel and performed the kind deed for them himself.

Brothers and sisters, take your little things to Christ—those trials of which your heart says, "They are too small. Though they prick me like thorns in the flesh and give me pain, they are really too trifling for me to mention in prayer." Not so! The Lord loves for you to trust him thoroughly. This is a token of his love, of his continued affection—that he will look even to the little things, that he will have compassion even on your small affairs. And you may ask him—oh, it is bold asking, but you may do it—to wash your feet, for he will do even that. We must believe in him so much that we can trust each day's cares to him, knowing that he still washes his disciples' feet by attending to our minor needs and griefs.

REFLECT

Are there any little things you need to bring to your Savior? What small thing are you struggling to believe Jesus cares about? Place each tiny worry in his helping hands.

PRAY

Jesus, you are so filled with love that you care for my soul and the dirt on the bottom of my feet. You tend to my eternity and my today. Nothing is too tiny, insignificant, or ordinary for your extraordinary grace. Lord, you know what I need more than I do—help me to receive your daily affection and attention. What a Savior! In your name, Lord. Amen.

DAY 31

Jesus Prays for Us

*Father, I desire that they also, whom you have
given me, may be with me where I am, to see
my glory that you have given me because you
loved me before the foundation of the world.*

JOHN 17:24

In this 17th chapter of John, we have, as it were, the
aroma of the Savior's priestly prayer. He prayed for
the people for whom he was about to die; before he
sprinkled them with his blood, he sanctified them with
his supplications. This prayer therefore stands preemi-
nent in holy Scripture as the Lord's prayer—the special
prayer of our Lord Jesus Christ. If one part of Scripture
can be dearer to the believer than any other, it must be
this, which contains our Master's last prayer before he
entered through the torn veil of his own crucified body.

The first thing he prayed for is that which is heav-
en's greatest joy: "Father, I desire that they also, whom
you have given me, may be with me where I am." If

you notice, every word in the sentence is necessary to its fullness. He does not say, *I pray that those, whom you have given me, may be where I am,* but he says, "with me where I am." Not only does he pray that we might be with him, but that we might be with him in the same place where he is. And notice that he did not say that he wished his people to be in heaven, but with him in heaven, because that makes heaven heaven. It is the very essence and marrow of heaven to be with Christ. Heaven without Christ would be an empty place. It would lose its happiness. It would be a harp without strings. Christ prayed that we might be with him—that is our companionship. And to be with him where he is—that is our position. He is showing us that heaven is both a condition and a location—in the company of Christ and in the place where Christ is.

The next prayer is for heaven's sweetest employment: "to see my glory that you have given me." I do not doubt that there are many joys which will amplify the grand joy we will have in heaven. I feel confident that the meeting of departed friends and the fellowship of apostles, prophets, priests, and martyrs will amplify the joy of the redeemed. But the sun that will shine the greatest light on our joy will be the fact that we are with Jesus Christ and behold his face. While there may be other employments in heaven, what is mentioned in the text is the chief one: "to see my glory."

Let us pass before our eyes the great scenes of glory which we shall behold after death. The moment the soul departs from this body, we will behold the glory of Christ. The glory of his person will be the first thing that will arrest our attention. He will sit on the throne, and our eyes will be caught with the glory of his appearance. Perhaps we shall be struck with astonishment. Is this the one that was more marred than any other man? Are these the hands that were once torn by iron? Is that the head that once was crowned with thorns? Is that the man who, scarred and bruised, was carried to his tomb? Is that the man who, for our salvation, conquered the grave? Yes, yes, yes!

Oh, how our admiration will rise and rise, and rise to the very highest pitch, when we will see the King of kings and Lord of lords. Christ prayed for you to see his glory, to be with him where he is, and be assured—his prayer will be answered.

REFLECT

What excites you most about heaven? How can you prepare your soul today to see the glory of Jesus? Remind yourself of his glory today.

PRAY

Lord Jesus, I respond in prayer to your prayer. I desire to be with you, where you are, that I may see the glory that the Father has given you. What a sight it will be! What a delight you are! Prepare my soul to savor the sight of my Savior. For your glory, Amen.

DAY 32

Remember Christ

*And he took bread, and when he had given
thanks, he broke it and gave it to them,
saying, "This is my body, which is given for
you. Do this in remembrance of me."*

LUKE 22:19

The main object of the Lord's Supper is evidently that
we should remember Christ by it. It is not that we
should call to mind a doctrine, though we should not be
ignorant or unmindful of any truth which the Spirit of
God has revealed. But the pith and essence of our business at his table is "Do this in remembrance of me": that
is, of himself—of his own blessed person. Think of him
not as an abstraction! Dream of him not as a mere idea!
Do not merely contemplate him as a historical person
who was once before people and has now passed from
the canvas of history, as Confucius, Aristotle, or the like.
No, he lives and abides—an actual, ever energetic force
and power among every generation. Jesus has that divine

nature that dwells perpetually in the present tense—the same yesterday, today, and forever.

You are taught that the very best way you can remember Christ is by receiving him. Oh, the sweetness of that truth if you will remember it when you come to this table! You are not asked to bring bread with you. It is here. You are not asked to bring a cup with you. It is here already provided. What do you have to do? Nothing but to eat and to drink. You have to be receivers and nothing more.

Now, whenever you want to remember your Lord and Master, you need not say, "I must do something for him." No, no, let him do something for you. O my brothers and sisters, come and receive; come and receive! You do not need to come with anything except your hunger and thirst. Someone that is invited to a meal need not say, "Oh, but I have no bread." You are invited to a royal feast, and you need not bring bread with you. He who invites you to his table will provide you with all you want, and when you desire to remember him, your surest and best plan is to enjoy the good things which he sets before you. Remember that you are healed by his stripes—think of those cruel scourges, those five wounds, that body covered with a bloody sweat, that thorn-encircled brow, and those eyes all dimmed with blood.

Christ's death is chosen for special celebration because it is the most important part of all that he did or suffered. We would not depreciate his life, his baptism, his work, or his resurrection, but his death is the center of all. All the doctrines of the gospel revolve around Christ's death, as the planets revolve around the sun. Take away the sun from the solar system, and you have dislocated everything. Remove your cross, O Christ, and the keystone of the arch of truth is gone! Take away your death, O Jesus, and it is death to all that you have taught—for all that you teach derives life from the fact that you indeed died! The dying of the Savior gives us life. His wounds heal us, his agonies bring us peace, and his tortures yield us ease. The good Shepherd knew that if his sheep desired to have green pastures, they would find them at the cross, so he appointed this sacrament to bring us there. Remember him, for he remembers you so as to be ever with you. For remember what your risen Christ says: "And behold, I am with you always, to the end of the age" (Matthew 28:20).

REFLECT

What five precious things do you want to remember about your Lord Jesus today? Spend a few minutes and meditate upon him.

PRAY

King Jesus, the bread and cup are now treasured tokens of your body on the cross and your blood shed for me. Gospel amnesia is a great spiritual disease. Keep me from it, Lord. May this supper quicken my memory of my Messiah. May I savor you, my Savior, above all. In your blood. Amen.

DAY 33

Great Drops of Blood

[Jesus said] "Father, if you are willing, remove this cup from me. Nevertheless, not my will, but yours, be done." And there appeared to him an angel from heaven, strengthening him. And being in agony he prayed more earnestly; and his sweat became like great drops of blood falling down to the ground.

LUKE 22:42-44

Our Lord, after having eaten and celebrated the Passover supper with his disciples, went with them to the Mount of Olives and entered the Garden of Gethsemane. What induced him to select that place to be the scene of his terrible agony? As in a garden Adam's self-indulgence ruined us, so in another garden the agonies of the second Adam should restore us. Gethsemane supplies the medicine for the ills which followed the forbidden fruit of Eden. It was in this garden where our Lord Jesus meant us to see that our sin changed everything about him into sorrow; it turned his riches into poverty, his peace into pain, his glory into shame. And so, in the place of his peaceful retirement, where in holy devotion he had been in communion with God, our sin transformed into the focus of his sorrow, the center of his woe.

His pleading in the garden became so fervent, so intense, that it forced from him a bloody sweat. We believe that, at this time, our Lord had a very clear view of all the shame and suffering of his crucifixion. The agony was just one of the first drops of the tremendous shower which discharged itself upon his head. He foresaw the speedy coming of the traitor-disciple, the seizure by the officers, the mock trials before the Sanhedrin and Pilate and Herod, the scourging and beating, the crown of thorns, the shame, the spitting. All these rose up before his mind, and, as it is a general law of our nature that the foresight of trial is more grievous than trial itself, we can conceive of how it was that he who did not speak a word when in the midst of the conflict could not restrain himself from strong crying and tears at the prospect of it. Beloved readers, if you can bring before your mind's eye the terrible incidents of his death—the hounding through the streets of Jerusalem, the nailing to the cross, the fever, the thirst, and, above all, the forsaking of his God—you cannot wonder that he began to be in great agony and physical weakness.

We see that Christ became exceedingly weak because an angel came from heaven to strengthen him—for the holy angels never do anything that is superfluous. But how strange it sounds to our ears that the Lord of life and glory would become so weak that he should need to be strengthened by one of his own creatures! How extraordinary it seems that he, who is "very God of very God," should, nevertheless, when he appeared on earth as Immanuel, so completely take on our nature that he should become so weak as to need to be sustained by angelic agency! Yet, this incident proves the reality of our Savior's human frailty.

Here you can perceive how fully he shares the weakness of our humanity—not in spiritual weakness, so as to become guilty of any sin, but in mental weakness, so as to be capable of great depression of spirit; and in physical weakness, so as to be exhausted to the last degree by his terrible bloody sweat. Learn the real humanity of our Lord Jesus Christ. Do not think of him as God only, though he is assuredly divine, but feel him to be close in likeness to you: bone of your bone, flesh of your flesh. How thoroughly he can sympathize with you! He has been burdened with all your burdens and grieved with all your griefs. Jesus can sympathize with you in all your sorrows, for he has suffered far more than you have ever suffered and is able to help you in your temptations. Take hold of Jesus as your familiar friend—your brother born for adversity—and you will have obtained a comfort which will bear you through the uttermost deeps.

REFLECT

What sorrows and temptations do you have today? Consider Jesus' blood on his brow and the real sympathy and comfort he has for you in this moment.

PRAY

Lord Jesus, I marvel at your commitment to me. You sweated drops of blood for my griefs, my sins, my redemption! May I never belittle the sins that brought you such sorrow. There is no match to your mercy. And there is no one who can sympathize with my weaknesses like you. I praise you, Jesus, my friend, born for adversity. Amen.

DAY 34

Christ Arrested

So the band of soldiers and their captain and the officers of the Jews arrested Jesus and bound him.

JOHN 18:12

Christ had scarcely risen from his knees, and the bloody sweat was like fresh ruby dew upon him, yet these men "arrested Jesus and bound him." Our only subject for today's reading is to consider Christ in shackles—the Son of God as an ambassador under arrest, a king in chains, the God-man sent and bound, to take his trial in the court of the high priest, Caiaphas.

It seems to me that this binding of our Lord shows, first, something of fear on the part of his captors. Why did they bind him? He would not attack them, and he had no desire to escape out of their hands. Yet they probably thought he might break loose from them or in some way outwit them. There is a latent, secret conviction in people's minds that the Christ is greater than he seems to be. Even when they attack him with their pagan weapons, they never seem to be satisfied with their own arguments, and they are continually seeking fresh ones. To this very day, the ungodly are afraid of Christ, and, often, their raging against him resembles the noise made by the boy who, when hurrying through the graveyard, whistles to keep his courage up.

They also bound Christ to increase the shame of his condition. Our Savior said to those who came to arrest him in the garden, "Have you come out as against a robber, with swords and clubs to capture me?" (Matthew 26:55). And now they bound him fast as though he were a thief—perhaps tied his hands with tight cords behind his back, to show that they regarded him as a felon and that they were not taking him into a civil court, where some case of law might be pending, but they already had condemned him by the very act of binding him. They treated him as if he were already sentenced and were not worthy to stand, a free man, and plead for himself before the judgment seat. Oh, what shame that the Lord of life and glory should be bound: that he, whom angels delight to worship, who is the very sun of their heaven, should yet be bound as though he were a felon and be sent away to be tried for his life!

From the binding of our Lord Jesus flows a fact that is its opposite: his people are all made free. When Christ was made a curse for us, he became a blessing to us. When Christ was made sin for us, we were made the righteousness of God in him. When he died, then we lived. And so, as he was bound, we are set free. That exchange of prisoners is seen in Barabbas being set free when the Lord Jesus Christ was given up to be crucified. Christ, the great Deliverer, has made you free, and you are "free indeed" (John 8:36). Enjoy your liberty. Enjoy access to God. Enjoy the privilege of claiming the promises which God has made to you. Enjoy the exercise of the power with which God has endowed you. Enjoy the holy anointing with which the Lord has prepared you for his service.

Do not sit and mope like a bird in a cage when you are free to soar away. Imagine a bird that has been in a cage for years, and then the cage is taken away—every wire of it. And yet, the poor thing has been so accustomed to sit on that perch inside the cage that it takes no notice of the fact that its prison is gone, and there it sits and mopes still. Fly away, sweet songbird! The green fields and the blue sky are all yours. Stretch your wings, soar away above the clouds, and sing the hymn of your freedom as though it would reach the ears of the angels. Let our spirits be this way, friends. Christ has set us free; therefore, let us not go back into slavery or sit still as though we were in prison. Let us rejoice in our liberty this very hour, and let us do so all our days.

REFLECT

What reactions does the humiliating arrest of Jesus stir in your heart? Where could you be living more freely in Christ than you are today?

PRAY

O Lord, those chains do not suit you! I cannot fathom the Holy One humiliated. Those chains belong to me, for I earned them with my sin. But in your grace, those rattling shackles sing of you being my substitute, paying my penalty, giving me eternal life. Praise you, Jesus. Amen.

DAY 35

Peter's Denials

*And after an interval of about an hour still
another insisted, saying, "Certainly this man
also was with him, for he too is a Galilean." But
Peter said, "Man, I do not know what you are
talking about." And immediately, while he was
still speaking, the rooster crowed. And the Lord
turned and looked at Peter. And Peter remembered
the saying of the Lord, how he had said to him,
"Before the rooster crows today, you will deny me
three times." And he went out and wept bitterly.*

LUKE 22:59-62

What was the reason for Peter's denial? First, it
was his fear of man. Bold Peter became an utter
coward. And, oh, how many have denied their Master
because they have been afraid of a jest or a jeer! It was
just a silly maid and another gossip with her and a few
idle serving-men and women around the outdoor fire,
but Peter was afraid of them, and therefore he was not

afraid to deny his Master. Perhaps the chief reason for Peter's denial of his Lord was his confidence in himself. If Peter had felt himself to be weaker, he would really have been stronger—but because he felt so strong in himself, he proved to be as weak as water and so denied his Master. What a mercy it was that Christ did not treat Peter as Peter treated him! Peter said, "I do not know him" (v 57). Ah, me! But if the blessed, meek, and lowly one had said, *I do not know him*, it would have been all over with Peter.

Consider the grace of Christ in looking at Peter, even in the midst of Peter's sin. Can you picture him up there in the hall, up yonder steps, before the high priest and the council? Peter is down below in the house, warming his hands at the fire. Can you see the Lord Jesus turning round and fixing his eyes intently upon his stumbling disciple? What do you see in that look? First, I see in that look that which makes me exclaim: what thoughtful love! Jesus is bound, he is accused, he has just been struck on the face, mocked and reviled, but his thoughts are of wandering Peter. Blessed be his dear name, Jesus always has an eye for his people whether he be in his shame or in his glory. Though now he reigns in glory, he still looks steadily upon his own; his delight is in them, and his care is over them. There was not a particle of selfishness about our Savior. I see, then, in our Lord's looking upon Peter a wondrously thoughtful love.

Christ's look was also one of inexpressible tenderness, as if the Master said by it, *I love you still, Peter. Come back to me, and I will yet restore you.* I think it was a heart-piercing look and a heart-healing look all in one. It was a look which revealed to Peter the darkness of his sin and also the tenderness of his Master's heart towards him. Possibly no words could have expressed all that was thrown into that look of compassion. I think a book as big as the Bible was contained within that look of Jesus. I invite all the tongues and all the pens in the world to tell us all that our divine Lord meant by that look. Our Savior employed the most prudent, the most comprehensive, the most useful method of speaking to the heart of his erring follower—he looked a library of love into him. His glance was a divine hieroglyph full of unutterable meanings, which it conveyed in a clearer and more vivid way than words could have done.

Remember today that, yes, Jesus still looks upon sinners. As the Lord looked upon Peter, so he looks upon you. He has not turned his back on you; he has not averted the gaze of his pity. He sees to the bottom of your heart and reads all your thoughts. You have no need to go far to find God—he is looking upon you. "He is actually not far from each one of us" (Acts 17:27). He is within eyesight. You are to look to him, and if you do, your eyes will meet his eyes, for already he looks upon you.

REFLECT

How does this look from Christ encourage your heart? Are there any denials of Christ in your life that need his restorative eyes?

PRAY

O Lord, I know Peter is not alone in this sin. How I have often denied knowing you with no evangelism, no prayer, no Bible-reading, no repentance, no heart-filled worship. Look upon me, King Jesus, forgive me, and restore me with your empowering eyes of love. Embolden my soul for the Savior I know and love. In your name. Amen.

DAY 36

Christ Mocked

And they stripped him and put a scarlet robe on him, and twisting together a crown of thorns, they put it on his head and put a reed in his right hand. And kneeling before him, they mocked him, saying, "Hail, King of the Jews!" And they spit on him and took the reed and struck him on the head. And when they had mocked him, they stripped him of the robe and put his own clothes on him and led him away to crucify him.

MATTHEW 27:28-31

Here is the Christ—the generous, loving, tender Christ—treated with indignity and scorn. We have before us a king, and such a king as was never known before. But see that scarlet robe—it is a contemptuous imitation of the imperial purple that a king wears. See that crown upon his head—it has rubies in it, but the rubies are composed of his own blood, forced from his blessed temples by the cruel thorns. They salute him with "Hail, King of the Jews!" but it is done in scorn.

The coronation of Christ with thorns has great meaning in it, for first it was a crown of triumph for Christ. Christ had fought with sin from the day when he stood foot to foot with it in the wilderness up to the time he entered Pilate's hall and had conquered it. As a witness that he had gained the victory, behold sin's crown seized as a trophy! What was the crown of sin? Thorns. They sprang from the curse, and now Christ has taken away its crown and put it on his own head. He has spoiled sin of its richest regalia, and he wears it himself. Glorious champion! All hail King Jesus!

Where I see the great substitute for sinners put to such shame, scorn, and ridicule, my heart says to itself, "See what sin deserves." There is nothing in the world that more richly deserves to be despised, abhorred, and condemned than sin. Think for a minute what sin is, and you will see that it deserves ridicule for its folly. What is sin? It is rebellion against the Omnipotent—a revolt against the Almighty. What utter folly that is! Let this crown of thorns serve as a mighty stimulus to your soul. First, for fervent love of him. Can you see him crowned with thorns and not be drawn to him? Worship him! Adore him! Bless him! And let your voices sing, "Worthy is the Lamb."

Next, we ought to be moved toward repentance. Did our sins put thorns around his head? Oh, my poor fallen nature. Let us declare before God our soul's grief that we should make the Savior suffer, and then let us pray for grace to hedge our lives around with thorns, that from this very day sin may not approach us.

Lastly, see how your Redeemer loved you. Recall when Christ stood by the grave of Lazarus and wept; the Jews said, "See how he loved him!" (John 11:36). Ah! But look at Christ there among those Roman soldiers—despised, rejected, insulted, ridiculed—and let me say to you, "See how he loved us—you, me, and all his people!" If I were to take all your love to Christ and heap it up like a vast mountain, and if I were to gather all the members of Christ's church on earth and tell them to empty their hearts, and then if I fetched out of heaven the multitudes of redeemed and perfected souls before the throne and they emptied their hearts— if I could collect all the love that ever has been and that ever shall be throughout eternity in all the saints—all that would be but a drop in a bucket compared with the boundless, fathomless love of Christ for us. So, friends, from this sad scene let us learn how greatly Jesus loved us, and let each one of us, in return, love him with all our heart.

REFLECT

What wells up in your heart and mind as you meditate on this passage and the sufferings of Christ for you? Contemplate the mighty love of Jesus.

PRAY

Lord, I am overwhelmed as I consider the sufferings you endured to redeem me. Your love for me let the crown of thorns pierce your head. Love let all the shame and mockery unfold. Infinite love overcame finite shame. I can never repay you, Jesus—but I love you and live for you. Praise you, my rock and Redeemer. Amen.

DAY 37

The Thief on the Cross

And he said, "Jesus, remember me when you come into your kingdom." And he said to him, "Truly, I say to you, today you will be with me in paradise."

LUKE 23:42-43

The story of the salvation of the dying thief is an example of the power of Christ to save, and of his abundant willingness to receive everyone that comes to him, in whatever plight they may be. What do you think must have converted this poor thief? It strikes me that it may have been—it must have been—the sight of our great Lord and Savior. And when the cross was lifted up, that thief hanging up on his own cross looked around, and I suppose he could see that inscription written in three languages: "Jesus of Nazareth, the King of the Jews" (John 19:19). If so, that writing was his little Bible, his New Testament, and he interpreted it by what he knew of the Old Testament. This dying thief also read the gospel out of the lips of

Christ's enemies. They said, "He saved others" (v 35). *Ah!* thought he. *Did he save others? Why should he not save me?* What a great bit of gospel that was for the dying thief! I think I could swim to heaven on that plank—"He saved others"—because if he saved others, he can surely save me.

Let's draw our attention to the sweet fact that the crucified thief was our Lord's last companion on earth. What so-called "sorry" company our Lord selected when he was here! He did not consort with the religious Pharisees or the philosopher Sadducees, but he was known as the "friend of tax collectors and sinners" (Matthew 11:19). How I rejoice at this! It gives me assurance that he will not refuse to associate with me. When the Lord Jesus made a friend of me, he certainly did not make a choice which brought him credit. Do you think he gained any honor when he made a friend of you? Has he ever gained anything by us? No, my friends. If Jesus had not stooped very low, he would not have come to me. And if he did not seek the most unworthy, he might not have come to you. You feel it so, and you are thankful that he came "not to call the righteous, but sinners" to repentance (Matthew 9:13).

I want you to notice that the last companion of Christ on earth was a sinner—and no ordinary sinner. He had broken even the laws of man, for he was a robber. And he was most likely the type of criminal that mixed murder with their robberies. He was probably a pirate in arms against the Roman government, making this a pretext for plundering as he had opportunity. At last he was arrested and was condemned by a Roman tribunal, which, on the whole, was usually just, and in this case was certainly just, for he himself confesses the justice of his condemnation. How striking that a convicted felon was the person with whom our Lord last spent time upon earth. What a lover of the souls of guilty men is he! What a stoop he makes to the very lowest of mankind! To this most unworthy of men, the Lord of glory spoke with matchless grace. He spoke to him such wondrous words as never can be excelled if you search the Scriptures through: "Today you will be with me in paradise."

Our Savior took this dying thief into the paradise of infinite delight, and this is where he will take all of us sinners who believe in him. If we are trusting him, we shall ultimately be with him in paradise. And the Lord put a time on the thief's ticket: "Today." The thief was near the gates of hell, but almighty mercy lifted him up. What a change from the cross to the crown—from the anguish of Calvary to the glory of the new Jerusalem! In those few hours, the thief was lifted from the dunghill and set among princes. Can you measure the change from that sinner, revolting in his iniquity when the sun was high at noon, to that same sinner—clothed in pure white and accepted in the Beloved—in the paradise of God when the sun went down? O glorious Savior, what marvels you can work!

REFLECT

What does the thief on the cross teach you about the reality of the gospel? How could this story of grace change the way you view others who may seem hopeless in their sin?

PRAY

Lord, you are mighty to save! You will embrace any sinner that comes to you. Even if we are in the midst of receiving the earthly penalty of our sins, the heavenly pardon from your voice sets us free from the eternal penalty. Thank you for making this sinner, me, your companion and friend. I love you, Jesus. Amen.

DAY 38

It Is Finished!

When Jesus had received the sour wine,
he said, "It is finished," and he bowed
his head and gave up his spirit.

JOHN 19:30

et the day unfold in your minds. Christ is brought
to the cross; he is nailed fast to the cruel wood. The
sun burns him. His brutal wounds increase the fever.
God forsakes him. "My God, my God, why have you
forsaken me?" (Matthew 27:47). While he hangs there
in mortal conflict with sin and Satan, his heart is broken; his limbs are dislocated. On and on he goes, steadily determined to drink the last dreg of that cup which
must not pass from him so his Father's will be done. At
last, he cries, "It is finished'! Christ dies. Hear it, Christians. Hear this shout of triumph as it rings today with
all the freshness and force which it had years ago! Hear
it from the sacred Word and from the Savior's lips, and

may the Spirit of God open your ears that you may understand what you hear!

What did the Savior mean by "It is finished"? First, that all the emblems, promises, prophecies, and Old Testament sacrifices were now fully realized in him. All the Scripture was now fulfilled. When he said, "It is finished," the whole book—from the first to the last, in both the law and the prophets—was finished in him. There is not a single jewel of promise or prophecy, from that first emerald which fell on the threshold of Eden to that last sapphire stone of Malachi, which was not set in the breastplate of the true High Priest.

When he said, "It is finished," Jesus totally destroyed the power of Satan, of sin, and of death—for you. The champion had entered the lists to do battle for our soul's redemption, against all our foes. He met Sin. Horrible, terrible, all but omnipotent Sin nailed Christ to the cross—but in that deed, Christ nailed Sin also to the tree. There they both did hang together—Sin and Sin's destroyer. Sin destroyed Christ, and by that destruction Christ destroyed Sin. The words "It is finished" consolidated heaven, shook hell, comforted earth, delighted the Father, glorified the Son, brought down the Spirit, and confirmed the everlasting covenant to all the chosen ones.

Dear friends, once more, take comfort from this finality, for the redemption of Christ's church is perfected. There is not another penny to be paid for her full release. There is no mortgage upon Christ's inheritance. Those whom he bought with blood are forever clear of all charges—paid for to the utmost. "It is finished"—finished forever. All those overwhelming debts, which would have sunk us to the lowest hell, have been discharged by the cross. And they who believe in Christ may appear with boldness even before the throne of God itself. "It is finished." Your sins have received their death blow; the robe of your righteousness has received its last thread. It is done—complete, perfect. It needs no addition; it can never suffer any diminution.

O Christian, do lay hold of this precious thought, for it is enough to make you leap though your legs were loaded with irons, and to make you sing though your mouth was mute. Oh, to think that we are perfectly accepted in Christ—that our justification is not partial; it does not go to a limited extent but goes the whole way. Oh, wondrous grace! As far as the east is from the west, so far has God removed our transgressions from us by the death of Christ (Psalm 103:12). This and this alone will put away sin. Therefore in this cross of Christ we glory; yes, and in it alone will we glory evermore.

REFLECT

How does the death of Jesus affect you? What do you want to express to the Lord Jesus today? What do you need to believe more firmly, eagerly, joyfully?

PRAY

O Lord, the scene of Good Friday is at the same time too painful and too wonderful for my heart. My soul is grieved and gladdened, lamenting and leaping, sorrowful and savoring all that happened on that bloody cross. I rejoice in my Redeemer! The wonder of grace! The freedom of forgiveness! Today, I drink of the sweet nectar of the gospel and say, "Thank you, Jesus!" Amen.

DAY 39

Christ and Sin Buried

*Now in the place where he was crucified there
was a garden, and in the garden a new tomb
in which no one had yet been laid. So because
of the Jewish day of Preparation, since the
tomb was close at hand, they laid Jesus there.*

JOHN 19:41-42

We are expressly told in holy Scripture that our Lord was buried. Why? Was it not, first, that we might have a certificate of his death? We do not bury living people. Further, the Lord Jesus would not have been buried if the centurion had not certified that he was certainly dead. The Roman officer had probably seen Christ's heart pierced by the soldier's spear, when blood and water flowed from his side. Christ's being given up for burial was Pilate's certificate that he had not merely pretended to die but that it was a real death and that his body had no life remaining in it. This is an essential point, for if Jesus did not die, he has made no atonement for sin. If he died not, then he rose not; and if he rose not, then your faith is in vain—you are still in your sins (1 Corinthians 15:17). The tomb, therefore, occupies a very important place in the story of the death of Jesus. Today, let us meditate on the burial of our Lord.

First, it was a new tomb where no remains had been previously laid; this would have removed the suspicion that another had arisen. And in this new tomb, no one could have claimed that Christ's body had touched the bones of some prophet or another holy man, and so came to life. As Christ was born of a virgin mother, so was he buried in a virgin tomb. Second, it was a rocky tomb, and therefore nobody could dig into it by night or tunnel through the earth and steal his body. It would seem, too, to be the proper thing for our Lord to have a tomb in a rock. You cannot fittingly put him in sand who is himself the Rock of Ages. No, let our Lord Jesus Christ, with that immutable love and eternal faithfulness of his, lie in the solid rock—the very kind of tomb that is wanted for him who is the Rock of our salvation.

And the spiritual application lies here—if our sins are to die, it must be with Christ. The best thing to do with our past sin, if it is indeed forgiven, is to bury it. We hope to see all our tendencies to sin killed and buried—buried so deep that not even a bone of a sin shall be left above ground. But first, sin must be to you a condemned, detestable thing, to be hunted down and put to death. Sin must really and truly be crucified. You will find you cannot kill the smallest viper in the nest of your heart if you get away from the cross. There is no death for sin except in the death of Christ. He took upon himself the whole load of our iniquities; he endured the entire weight of the crushing burden, and by his atoning death he cast our iniquities into the depths of the sea. In the tomb of Jesus, all our sins are buried. Christ himself has put them away, and they can never rise against us in judgment anymore. Let none of you labor under that fear. Your old sins are buried, and they shall never have a resurrection.

REFLECT

What would change in your heart and daily life if you saw your sins as buried and left behind in the garden tomb? Where do you need to experience God's forgiveness?

PRAY

Father, I see the grave of the beloved Son, my Lord and Savior, and I see my sin, guilt, and shame laid to rest. Today, in real time, I can enjoy forgiveness, justification, and no condemnation because Christ died and was buried—and because I know Sunday's coming. In the name above every name. Amen.

DAY 40

He Is Risen!

He is not here, for he has risen, as he said.
Come, see the place where he lay.

MATTHEW 28:6

The resurrection of Christ is vital because it tells us that the gospel is the gospel of a living Savior. Let it be known and understood that foundational to our faith is that Christ's very limbs, which lay stiff and cold in death, became warm with life again. The silent heart began to beat again, and through the stagnant canals of the veins, the lifeblood began to circulate. The soul of the Redeemer again took possession of the body, and he lived once more. Let it be known that the very body which lay there, with its bones and blood and flesh, became again animated with life and came forth into a glorious existence. He was no phantom—no illusion. Jesus is a real man in glory now, even as he was when here below. Now, we always want to have that doctrine stated to us plainly, for though we believe it, we do not always realize it. And even if we have realized it, it is good to hear it again, to confirm it in our minds.

The doctrine of a risen Savior is exceedingly precious. The resurrection is the cornerstone of the entire building of Christianity. It is the keystone of the arch of our salvation. When our Lord Jesus rose from the dead, after having died, he had fully paid the penalty that was due to justice for the sin of his people, and his new life was a life clear of penalty, free from liability. You and I are clear from the claims of the law because Jesus stood in our stead, and God will not exact payment both from us and from our substitute.

And now, joy upon joy! He who took our debt has now delivered himself from it by dying on the cross. His new life, now that he has risen from the dead, is a life free from legal claim, and it is the token to us, whom he represented, that we are free also. Listen! "Who shall bring any charge against God's elect? It is God who justifies. Who is to condemn? Christ Jesus is the one who died—more than that, who was raised" (Romans 8:33-34). Fear takes a knockdown blow when the apostle says we cannot be condemned because Christ has died in our stead—but he puts a double force into it when he cries, "More than that, who was raised…" If Satan should come to any believer and say, "What about your sin?" tell him that Jesus died for it, and your sin is put away. If he asks a second time, answer him, "Jesus lives, and his life is the assurance of our justification."

Remember your risen Lord and how he cares for you. Do weaknesses hinder you? The living Christ will show himself strong on your behalf. You have a living Christ, and in him you have all things. Do you dread death? Jesus, in rising again, has vanquished the last enemy. He will come and meet you when it is your turn to pass through the chill stream, and you shall cross it in sweet company. What is your trouble? No matter what it is, if you will only think of Jesus as living, full of power, full of love, and full of sympathy, having experienced all your trials even unto death, you will have such a confidence in his tender care and in his boundless ability that you will follow in his footsteps without a question. Remember Jesus and that he rose again from the dead, and your confidence will rise as on eagles' wings.

Today, in some way or other, I pray you make known that Jesus Christ is risen. Pass the news around, as the ancient Christians did. On the first day of the week, they said to one another, "The Lord is risen indeed." If anyone asks what you mean by it, you will then be able to tell them the whole gospel. For this is the essence of the gospel: that Jesus Christ died for our sins and rose again on the third day, according to the Scriptures. He died as the substitute for us criminals and rose as the representative of us pardoned sinners; he died that our sins might die and lives again that our souls may live.

REFLECT

Is the reality of the risen Christ more precious to you today? How will you live in light of the risen King? Who needs to hear from you that the Lord is risen indeed?

PRAY

My risen King, your heart beats, and it defeats my sins, the devil, and death. I trust in your blood spilled at the cross and the blood that courses through your veins in heaven at this very moment. Because you live, I can face yesterday, today, and tomorrow. All hail, the risen King! What a happy Easter! In your name, Jesus. Amen.

APPENDIX

If you are interested in reading the sermons I drew upon for these devotionals, the appendix below will point you to the corresponding sermon from Spurgeon. While Spurgeon's sermons are widely available online, you may find the search bar at Spurgeon.org to be a simple way to look for them. "The Spurgeon Archive" at romans45.org also has Spurgeon's sermons listed in alphabetical order.

DAY 1
"The Baptist's Message"
"Behold the Lamb of God"

DAY 2
"Lessons from Christ's Baptism"

DAY 3
"Tempted of the Devil"
"Temptations on the Pinnacle"

DAY 4
"Christ's First and Last Subject"

DAY 14
"The Christ-Given Rest"
"Christ's Word with You"
"The Meek and Lowly One"
"The Heart of Jesus"
"The Old Gospel for the New Century"

DAY 15
"Compassion for the Multitude"

DAY 16
"Good Cheer from Christ's Real Presence"
"Jesus No Phantom"

DAY 17
"Peter's Shortest Prayer"

DAY 18
"The One Thing Needful"

DAY 19
"Our Own Dear Shepherd"

DAY 20
"Christ's Transfigured Face"
"Jesus Only"

DAY 21
"Hope in Hopeless Cases"

DAY 22
"A Greater Than Solomon"

DAY 23
"Counting the Cost"

DAY 24
"The Reception of Sinners"
"Prodigal Love for the Prodigal Son"

DAY 25
"Christ the Seeker and Saviour of the Lost"
"The Mission of the Son of Man"
"Good News for the Lost"
"The Errand of Mercy"

DAY 26
"The Redeemer's Face Set Like a Flint"

DAY 27
"Hosanna!"
"The Triumphal Entry into Jerusalem"
"An Exciting Enquiry"

DAY 28
"I Would; but Ye Would Not"

DAY 29
"Concentration and Diffusion"

DAY 30
"The Teaching of the Foot-Washing"
"Jesus Washing His Disciples' Feet"

DAY 31
"The Redeemer's Prayer"

DAY 32
"The Lord's Supper: A Remembrance of Jesus"
"The Lord's Supper"

DAY 33
"The Weakened Christ Strengthened"
"Gethsemane"
"The Agony in Gethsemane"
"Christ in Gethsemane"

DAY 34
"Christ in Bonds"

DAY 35
"Peter's Fall and Restoration"
"Peter's Restoration"

DAY 36
"The Crown of Thorns"
"Mocking the King"
"Mocked of the Soldiers"

DAY 37

"The Dying Thief in a New Light"
"The Believing Thief"

DAY 38

"None but Jesus—Second Part"
"Three Crosses"
"Christ's Dying Word for His Church"
"It Is Finished!"

DAY 39

"The Old Man Crucified"
"Over against the Sepulchre"
"A Royal Funeral"
"The Rule of the Race"

DAY 40

"The Resurrection of Our Lord Jesus"
"A Visit to the Tomb"
"Jesus Appearing to Mary Magdalene"
"The Stone Rolled Away"

365 DAILY DEVOTIONS

A year of gospel-saturated daily devotions from renowned Bible teacher Alistair Begg. Reflecting on a short passage each day, Alistair spans the Scriptures to show us the greatness and grace of God, and to thrill our hearts to live as his children. This resource will both engage your mind and stir your heart.

thegoodbook.com/daily-truth1
thegoodbook.co.uk/daily-truth1
thegoodbook.com.au/daily-truth1

UNDERSTANDING CALVINISM
IN OUR HEARTS

A warm-hearted, accessible introduction to the five points of Calvinism, showing how a true understanding of them can make you a more humble and loving Christian. Author Jeff Medders shows how taking Calvinism to heart should fuel a love of Christ and his people that builds others up.

thegoodbook.com/humble-calvinism
thegoodbook.co.uk/humble-calvinism
thegoodbook.com.au/humble-calvinism

thegoodbook
COMPANY

BIBLICAL | RELEVANT | ACCESSIBLE

At The Good Book Company we are dedicated to helping Christians and local churches grow. We believe that God's growth process always starts with hearing clearly what he has said to us through his timeless and flawless word—the Bible.

Ever since we opened our doors in 1991, we have been striving to produce resources that are biblical, relevant, and accessible. By God's grace, we have grown to become an international publisher, encouraging ordinary Christians of every age and stage and every background and denomination to live for Christ day by day and equipping churches to grow in their knowledge of God, their love for one another, and the effectiveness of their outreach.

Call one of our friendly team for a discussion of your needs or visit one of our local websites for more information on the resources and services we provide.

Your friends at The Good Book Company

thegoodbook.com | thegoodbook.co.uk
thegoodbook.com.au | thegoodbook.co.nz
thegoodbook.co.in